A Note From Rick Renner

I am on a personal quest to see a "revival of the Bible" so people can establish their lives on a firm foundation that will stand strong and endure the test when the end-time storm winds begin to intensify.

In order to experience a revival of the Bible in your personal life, it is important to take time each day to read, receive, and apply its truths to your life. James tells us that if we will continue in the perfect law of liberty — refusing to be forgetful hearers but determined to be doers — we will be blessed in our ways. As you watch or listen to the programs in this series and work through this corresponding study guide, I trust that you will search the Scriptures and allow the Holy Spirit to help you hear something new from God's Word that applies specifically to your life. I encourage you to be a doer of the Word that He reveals to you. Whatever the cost, I assure you — it will be worth it.

> Thy words were found, and I did eat them;
> and thy word was unto me the joy and rejoicing of mine heart:
> for I am called by thy name, O Lord God of hosts.
> — Jeremiah 15:16

Your brother and friend in Jesus Christ,

Rick Renner

Qualifications for Leadership

Copyright © 2020 by Rick Renner
8316 E. 73rd St.
Tulsa, Oklahoma 74133

Published by Rick Renner Ministries
www.renner.org

ISBN 13: 978-1-6803-1-677-3

eBook ISBN 13: 978-1-6803-1-682-7

How To Use This Study Guide

This ten-lesson study guide corresponds to *"Qualifications for Leadership" With Rick Renner* (**Renner TV**). Each lesson in this study guide covers a topic that is addressed during the program series, with questions and references supplied to draw you deeper into your own private study of the Scriptures on this subject.

To derive the most benefit from this study guide, consider the following:

First, watch or listen to the program prior to working through the corresponding lesson in this guide. (Programs can also be viewed at **renner.org** by clicking on the Media/Archives links.)

Second, take the time to look up the scriptures included in each lesson. Prayerfully consider their application to your own life.

Third, use a journal or notebook to make note of your answers to each lesson's Study Questions and Practical Application challenges.

Fourth, invest specific time in prayer and in the Word of God to consult with the Holy Spirit. Write down the scriptures or insights He reveals to you about being filled with the Spirit and empowered by Him in your daily life.

Finally, take action! Whatever the Lord tells you to do according to His Word, do it.

For added insights on this subject, it is recommended that you obtain Rick Renner's book *Promotion: Ten Guidelines To Help You Achieve Your Long Awaited Promotion*. You may also select from Rick's other available resources by placing your order at **renner.org** or by calling 1-800-742-5593.

TOPIC

A Leadership Crisis

SCRIPTURES

1. **Acts 20:28-31** — Take heed therefore unto yourselves, and to all the flock, over the which the Holy Ghost hath made you overseers, to feed the church of God, which he hath purchased with his own blood. For I know this, that after my departing shall grievous wolves enter in among you, not sparing the flock. Also of your own selves shall men arise, speaking perverse things, to draw away disciples after them. Therefore watch, and remember, that by the space of three years I ceased not to warn every one night and day with tears.

GREEK WORDS

1. "hath made" — τίθημι (*tithemi*): to set, fix, establish, or position

2. "overseers" — ἐπίσκοπος (*episkopos*): one who watches, looks, observes, or surveys; one who has oversight or who administrates or manages; a supervisory position; pictures a ruler entrusted with the care of a city or country; depicts a political leader who was to provide oversight and management of a region and of all the citizens who lived in that region; depicts construction supervisors who provided oversight of construction sites, ensuring that funds were spent properly, that expenditures didn't exceed the budget, that people did their jobs correctly, and that construction of a building was done in compliance with the desires of the architect; pictures one whose task is to give oversight and who is ultimately responsible for an entire project from beginning to end; used to describe official administrative officials in the city of Athens; a bishop

3. "I know" — ἐγὼ οἶδα (*ego oida*): from the words ἐγώ (*ego*) and οἶδα (*oida*); the word ἐγώ (*ego*) emphatically means "I" and is where we get the word ego; by using this word, Paul made an emphatic statement stressing himself and his own position; the word οἶδα (*oida*) means to know, perceive, understand, or comprehend; literally, "I...I, know"

4. "after" — μετά (*meta*): after; pointing to a subsequent moment

5. "departing" — **ἄφιξις** (*aphixis*): a departure; a release; "after vacating my post and departing"

6. "grievous" — **βαρύς** (*barus*): plural, burdensome, heavy, imposing, weighty; cruel, oppressive, severe, stern, unsparing, violent; pictures one who used oppressive force; one who presses down on another; one who manipulates and whose objective is to dominate and take control

7. "wolves" — **λύκος** (*lukos*): plural form in context; a wolf or jackal; used to depict wolfish individuals who come to attack, victimize, and take advantage of others

8. "among you" — **εἰς ὑμᾶς** (*eis humas*): right into your midst; right among you

9. "not sparing" — **μὴ φειδόμενοι** (*me pheidomenoi*): the words **μή** (*me*) and **φείδομαι** (*pheidomai*); the word **μή** (*me*) means "emphatically not"; the word **φείδομαι** (*pheidomai*) means to spare or to treat something leniently; in this verse, "will not spare" or "will not treat leniently"; will not treat with care, will not treat kindly; hence, abuse, exploitation, and ill-treatment

10. "of your own selves" — **ἐξ ὑμῶν αὐτῶν** (*ex humon auton*): right out of your own company; right out of your own selves; from your own very midst

11. "arise" — **ἀνίστημι** (*anistemi*): to stand up; to rise up; to appear

12. "speaking" — **λαλοῦντες** (*lalountes*): a form of **λαλέω** (*laleo*); to speak or to converse

13. "perverse" — **διαστρέφω** (*diastrepho*): in context, twisted; twisted into a new shape; distorted; perverted; hence, corrupted

14. "draw away" — **ἀποσπάω** (*apospao*): to draw away; to tear away; to wrench away; often indicates an emotional wrenching away

15. "watch" — **γρηγορέω** (*gregoreo*): to be on your guard; denotes the watchful attitude of one who is on the lookout to make certain no enemy or aggressor can successfully gain entry into his life or place of residence; to be on high alert; depicts a person whose attitude is to never let up; to be watchful and wide awake to make certain a sinister force doesn't sneak up to attack and overtake him

16. "tears" — **δάκρυον** (*dakruon*): plural in this text; simply, tears; nonstop tears

SYNOPSIS

The ten lessons in this study on *Qualifications for Leadership* will focus on the following topics:

- A Leadership Crisis
- What Is a Bishop?
- Desire
- Blameless
- The Husband of One Wife
- Vigilant, Sober, Good Behavior, Hospitality, Apt To Teach
- Not Addicted, No Striker
- Patient, Not a Brawler, Not Covetous
- Rules Well His Own Home, Respectable Children
- Not a Novice, Good Reputation With Unbelievers

The emphasis of this lesson:

Good leaders are needed in every sphere of life — including in the Church. After Paul left the church of Ephesus, corrupt leaders arose right from among the existing leadership, just as he had predicted.

The ancient city of Ephesus was absolutely magnificent during the First Century. It featured a luxurious marketplace and a beautiful basilica etched with decorative frescos, ornate mosaics, and carved columns. Just a stone's throw from there was a place called the Bouleuterion, which was where the city council assembled regularly. The leaders who served in this prestigious group governed the city, deciding all its policies and ruling on all issues that arose in their jurisdiction.

What's interesting is that the city of Ephesus was also home to the world's largest church, and Timothy served as its pastor. Unfortunately, many of the church leaders had gotten off track into doctrinal error, creating a serious leadership crisis. In an effort to fill the void, the apostle Paul gave Timothy a list of qualifications for selecting new leaders to serve in their place. These are the same qualifications we, too, must adhere to in order to serve in positions of spiritual leadership.

Paul's Final Farewell to the Ephesian Leaders

After Paul had firmly established the church of Ephesus, a great political disturbance arose in the city that forced him to leave and not return. As he made his way to Jerusalem, he called for the elders in Ephesus to meet with him one last time in the nearby city of Miletus. In his final farewell to the church leaders he said, "Take heed therefore unto yourselves, and to all the flock, over the which the Holy Ghost hath made you overseers, to feed the church of God, which he hath purchased with his own blood" (Acts 20:28).

Notice the phrase "take heed." It is the Greek word *prosecho*, which in this case means *to give one's full attention to a matter* or *to apply the mind to a thing*. By using this word, Paul was urging the leaders to be very mindful of their spiritual condition and give their full attention to taking care of it. This same instruction applies to us. If we fail to take care of ourselves and become depleted, we won't have what we need to help anyone else.

Once we are mindfully caring for our own spiritual well-being, then we are in a position to care for others, which is what Paul told the Ephesian elders. He said they were to care for "…all the flock, over the which the Holy Ghost hath made you overseers…" (Acts 20:28). The words "hath made" are from the Greek word *tithemi*, which means *to set, fix, establish*, or *position*. Essentially, Paul was reminding the elders that it was the Holy Spirit who had *established* and *positioned* them as leaders. The Spirit of God had set them in their ruling place, and they were accountable to Him.

The Bible says their job was to be "overseers," which in Greek is the word *episkopos*, and it describes *one who watches, looks, observes, or surveys; one who has oversight or who administrates or manages.* This is *a supervisory position* and pictures *a ruler entrusted with the care of a city or country*. It can also picture *a political leader who was to provide oversight and management of a region and of all the citizens who lived in that region.*

Furthermore, the word *episkopos* — translated here as "overseers" — has been used to depict *construction supervisors who provided oversight of construction sites, ensuring that funds were spent properly, that expenditures didn't exceed the budget, that people did their jobs correctly, and that construction of a building was done in compliance with the desires of the architect.* This word can also picture *one whose task is to give oversight and who is ultimately responsible for an entire project from beginning to end.* It was a legal term used to describe administrative officials in the city of Athens. In the New Testament, the word *episkopos* is often translated as the word "bishop," which encompasses anyone who serves as an administrator or supervisor within the church.

Spiritual 'Wolves' Would Arise After Paul Departed

Paul went on to say, "For I know this, that after my departing shall grievous wolves enter in among you, not sparing the flock" (Acts 20:29). Normally, the words "I know" in Greek is the word *oida*, which means *I know, I understand,* or *I comprehend.* Yet in this verse, "I know" is a translation of two words: *ego oida.* The word *ego* emphatically means "I" and is where we get the word "ego." By including this term, Paul made an emphatic statement stressing himself and his own position. The word *oida* means *to know, perceive, understand,* or *comprehend.* Thus Paul was literally saying, "I…I emphatically know."

What did Paul emphatically know? That spiritual wolves would enter in among the people "after" he departed. The word "after" is the Greek word *meta*, which means *after* and it points to *a subsequent moment.* The word "departing" is the Greek word *aphixis*, and it describes *a departure* or *a release.* Paul was specifically referring to *the timeframe after he vacated his post and departed.*

This brings us to the word "wolves," which is taken from the Greek word *lukos.* It describes *a wolf or jackal.* Here it is used to depict *wolfish individuals who come to attack, victimize, and take advantage of others.* And Paul said these wolfish individuals would be "grievous," which is the Greek word *barus.* It means *burdensome, heavy, imposing, weighty;* it describes one who is *cruel, oppressive, severe, stern, unsparing,* or *violent.* It pictures *one who used oppressive force; one who presses down on another; or one who manipulates and whose objective is to dominate and take control.*

Paul warned the Ephesian elders that the wolves would "…enter in among you, not sparing the flock" (Acts 20:29). The words "among you" is *eis humas* in Greek, which means *right into your midst; right among you.* The phrase "not sparing" is *me pheidomenoi* in the Greek. The word *me* means *emphatically not,* and the word *pheidomai* means *to spare* or *to treat something leniently.* In this verse, it indicates *they will not spare or will not treat leniently; they will not treat with care; they will not treat kindly.* Hence, these ravenous individuals will abuse, exploit, and mistreat the believers.

Why didn't the wolves show up when Paul was still present? The reason is, they were afraid of Paul and knew he would expose them, rebuke them, and not tolerate any of their manipulative ploys. Make no mistake: where there are strong spiritual leaders, much of the nonsense that goes on in churches is squashed before it has a chance to start.

Wolves Speak 'Perverse Things'

One of the most alarming aspects about Paul's warning to the leaders in Ephesus is the place from which the wolves would arise. He said, "Also of your own selves shall men arise, speaking perverse things, to draw away disciples after them" (Acts 20:30). The phrase "of your own selves" in Greek is *ex humon auton,* which means *right out of your own company; right out of your own selves.* In other words, *from your own very midst,* these wolves would "arise."

The word "arise" is *anistemi* in the Greek, which means *to stand up; to rise up;* or *to appear.* Paul predicted that men *right from among their own company* would suddenly stand up and begin "speaking perverse things." The word "speaking" is the Greek word *lalountes,* which is a form of *laleo,* meaning *to speak or to converse;* and the word "perverse" in Greek is the word *diastrepho,* which in context means *twisted.* Wolves take the truth and *twist it into a new shape.* What they speak is *distorted, perverted,* and *corrupted.*

Basically, Paul predicted that once he left his post as the leading apostle in Ephesus, cruel and oppressive individuals would arise and begin to twist and distort the truth of the Gospel for their own personal gain. Specifically, Paul said they would "…draw away disciples after them" (Acts 20:30). The phrase "draw away" is the Greek word *apospao,* which means *to draw away; to tear away;* or *to wrench away.* It often indicates *an emotional wrenching away.* The teaching of these corrupt spiritual leaders would create an emotional catastrophe for the believers in Ephesus.

Paul Urged the Leaders To Be 'Watchful'

To combat the efforts of the "wolves," Paul instructed the Ephesian elders to "watch." He wrote, "Therefore watch, and remember, that by the space of three years I ceased not to warn every one night and day with tears"

(Acts 20:31). The word "watch" is the Greek word *gregoreo*, which means *to be on your guard*. It denotes *the watchful attitude of one who is on the lookout to make certain no enemy or aggressor can successfully gain entry into his life or place of residence*. It also means *to be on high alert*. The word *gregoreo* depicts *a person whose attitude is to never let up; to be watchful and wide awake to make certain a sinister force doesn't sneak up to attack and overtake him* or what he is guarding.

What Paul was instructing the elders to do, he himself had done for three years — with "tears." This word "tears" is a translation of the Greek word *dakruon*, which is plural in this text and simply means *nonstop tears*. Before his departure, Paul had painstakingly forewarned the leaders in Ephesus day and night for three years that the enemy would attempt to invade their ranks. They were to be on high alert, watching with eyes wide open to guard against those attacks.

As predicted, after Paul's departure, the enemy eventually did invade the church of Ephesus through these deceptive leaders. Timothy was in the midst of a major leadership crisis, which is why Paul wrote to him and told him to remove the corrupt leaders and select new leaders from among the people. He then gave Timothy a list of qualifications for any person who aspired to serve in any level of leadership in the church. We will focus on these qualifications in the coming lessons.

STUDY QUESTIONS

Study to shew thyself approved unto God, a workman that needeth not to be ashamed, rightly dividing the word of truth.
— 2 Timothy 2:15

1. Good leaders make a powerful impact on the people they serve. From your perspective, who would you say is an example of *a good leader* — past or present — in *the Church*? How about in *the civic* or *governmental* arenas? How about in *the family*?

2. Looking at the individuals you have named, what character qualities do you see in them that makes them good leaders? What do you admire most about these people?

3. What very important principle about being promoted to a place of leadership is found in Psalm 75:6,7? How about in Matthew 25:21,23?

PRACTICAL APPLICATION

But be ye doers of the word, and not hearers only,
deceiving your own selves.
—James 1:22

The truth is, all of us — including *you* — are leading someone. Right now, there are people in your life who are watching what you do and listening to what you say, and it is influencing their lives.

1. Stop and think about it. Whom has the Lord positioned over you in a place of leadership? Whom are *you* leading, and how are you leading them?

2. As a leader, you cannot give away what you don't have. Therefore, to help strengthen others, you have to maintain your own spiritual strength. Are you reading and studying the Bible? Are you praying, and are you praying in the language of the Spirit? What practical steps do you know you need to take to grow and to strengthen yourself spiritually?

LESSON 2

TOPIC

What Is a Bishop?

SCRIPTURES

1. **1 Timothy 1:3,6** — As I besought thee to abide still at Ephesus, when I went into Macedonia, that thou mightest charge some that they teach no other doctrine.... From which some having swerved have turned aside unto vain jangling.

2. **1 Timothy 3:1-7** — This is a true saying, If a man desire the office of a bishop, he desireth a good work. A bishop then must be blameless, the husband of one wife, vigilant, sober, of good behaviour, given to hospitality, apt to teach; not given to wine, no striker, not greedy of filthy lucre; but patient, not a brawler, not covetous; one that ruleth well his own house, having his children in subjection with all gravity; (for if a man know not how to rule his own house, how shall he

take care of the church of God?) Not a novice, lest being lifted up with pride he fall into the condemnation of the devil. Moreover he must have a good report of them which are without; lest he fall into reproach and the snare of the devil.

3. **Galatians 3:28** — There is neither Jew nor Greek, there is neither bond nor free, there is neither male nor female: for ye are all one in Christ Jesus.

GREEK WORDS

1. "besought" — **παρακαλέω** (*parakaleo*): urge, beseech, plead, beg, or pray; used to depict military leaders who came alongside their troops to urge, exhort, beseech, beg, and plead with them to stand tall and face their battles bravely

2. "charge" — **παραγγέλλω** (*parangello*): to charge; to command; to give an order; to strictly command

3. "no other doctrine" — **ἑτεροδιδασκαλέω** (*heterodidaskaleo*): compound of **ἕτερος** (*heteros*) and **διδάσκαλος** (*didaskalos*); the word **ἕτερος** (*heteros*) means "of a different kind," and it emphasizes something that is qualitatively different from its counterpart; the word **διδάσκαλος** (*didaskalos*) means "teaching"; when the two words are compounded, the new word means "teachings of a different kind," indicating incorrect teaching; teaching that is qualitatively different from correct teaching

4. "swerved" — **ἀστοχέω** (*astocheo*): to miss the mark; to be off target; to be out of line; to deviate from the goal or from truth

5. "turned aside" — **ἐκτρέπω** (*ektrepo*): to turn away; also, a medical term that describes a bone out of joint; depicts wandering from an originally intended location; a mutation into something different than originally intended

6. "vain jangling" — **ματαιολογία** (*mataiologia*): wasted talk; empty words; foolish, nonsensical talk; useless chatter

7. "true" — **πιστὸς** (*pistos*): faithful; reliable; dependable; trustworthy

8. "a man" — **τις** (*tis*): anyone; either male or female; it is not specific to male or female

9. "desire" — **ὀρέγω** (*orego*): to stretch forward; to reach toward; the longing, cravings, urge, burning desire, or yearning ambition to achieve something or to become something; it portrays a person so

fixed on the object of his desire that his entire being is stretched forward to take hold of that goal or object

10. "office of a bishop" — ἐπίσκοπος (*episkopos*): one who watches, looks, observes, or surveys; one who has oversight or who administrates or manages; a supervisory position; pictures a ruler entrusted with the care of a city or country; depicts a political leader who was to provide oversight and management of a region and of all the citizens who lived in that region; depicts construction supervisors who provided oversight of construction sites, ensuring that funds were spent properly, that expenditures didn't exceed the budget, that people did their jobs correctly, and that construction of a building was done in compliance with the desires of the architect; pictures one whose task is to give oversight and who is ultimately responsible for an entire project from beginning to end; used to describe official administrative officials in the city of Athens; a bishop

SYNOPSIS

As we saw in our first lesson, the ancient city of Ephesus was home to the Bouleuterion. The word "Bouleuterion" is from the word *boules*, which means *to counsel*. Thus the Bouleuterion was a place where all the city councilors met to discuss issues, policies, and problems. To be selected to serve in this illustrious group, one had to have a spotless reputation.

Similarly, if we are going to serve as leaders in God's house, we are going to have a good reputation. We have to meet God's qualifications and have good-standing among believers and non-believers alike. These reputable people are the kind of leaders the apostle Paul instructed Timothy to look for when a leadership crisis arose in the church of Ephesus.

Paul said, "This is a true saying, If a man desire the office of a bishop, he desireth a good work" (1 Timothy 3:1). What's interesting is that the word "bishop" was actually a secular term in the First Century and had no religious connection whatsoever. It was used to describe anyone who stood in a leadership position.

The emphasis of this lesson:

The word "bishop" is one of the terms for a leader mentioned in Scripture. Although it seems religious in nature, in the First Century it was

a common, secular term. Paul used this word when he charged Timothy to choose new, qualified leaders to serve in the church.

Paul Urged Timothy To Deal With the Perverted Leaders

When Paul spoke his final farewell to the elders in Ephesus, he predicted with pinpoint precision what would happen once he disconnected with his spiritual position there: He said spiritual "wolves" would arise from among the people in the church, twisting the truth of the Gospel in order to draw people to themselves, and that is exactly what took place.

To deal with this destabilizing dilemma, Paul told Timothy who was pastoring the church, "As I besought thee to abide still at Ephesus, when I went into Macedonia, that thou mightest charge some that they teach no other doctrine" (1 Timothy 1:3).

To understand what Paul was saying here, we need to examine some of the key words in this verse. First, notice the word "besought." It is the Greek word *parakaleo*, and it means *to urge, beseech, plead, beg, or pray*. This word was used to depict *military leaders who came alongside their troops to urge, exhort, beseech, beg, and plead with them to stand tall and face their battles bravely*. Timothy was facing a battle. There were people with ulterior motives trying to position themselves as leaders in the church of Ephesus. Paul came alongside Timothy and *begged* and *pleaded* with him to accept the assignment to identify these twisted leaders and remove them.

Sometimes in life you just have to face the conflict in front of you whether you like it or not. You need to throw your shoulders back, hold your head high, and deal with the issues head-on. As you do, remember that God has joined Himself to you and you can conquer whatever is in front you.

The Bible says Paul gave Timothy a "charge" to deal with these perverted leaders. The word "charge" is the Greek word *parangello*, which means *to charge; to command; to give an order;* or *to strictly command*. The order Paul gave was "...that they teach no other doctrine" (1 Timothy 1:3). The phrase "no other doctrine" is a translation of the Greek word *heterodidaskaleo*. It is a compound of the word words *heteros* and *didaskalos*. The word *heteros* means *of a different kind*, and it emphasizes *something that is qualitatively different from its counterpart*. The word *didaskalos* means *teaching*. When these two words are compounded, the new word means *teachings of a different kind.* It indicates *incorrect teaching* or *teaching that is qualitatively different from correct teaching.*

The wolfish individuals who arose right from among the congregation in the church of Ephesus were taking the pure Word of God and distorting it to say what they wanted it to say in order "…to draw away disciples after them" (Acts 20:30). By adding a slightly new twist to the revelation of truth that others were teaching — thereby polluting or corrupting it — they effectively grabbed people's attention and got people to listen.

Corrupt Leaders Are Like 'a Bone Out of Joint'

Paul declared these people to be charlatans, which "…having swerved have turned aside unto vain jangling" (1 Timothy 1:6). The word "swerved" is the Greek term *astocheo*, which means *to miss the mark; to be off target; to be out of line;* or *to deviate from the goal or from truth.* Moreover, the phrase "turned aside" is a translation of the Greek word *ektrepo,* meaning *to turn away.* It depicts *wandering from an originally intended location* or *a mutation into something different than originally intended.*

What is interesting is the word *ektrepo* was also *a medical term that describes a bone out of joint.* If you have ever dislocated your shoulder, your knee, or another bone, you know how much pain it can create. By using the word *ektrepo,* the Holy Spirit is saying that just as one bone out of joint sends signals of pain to the entire body and affects your ability to function normally, one leader that is spiritually "out of joint" sends signals of pain to the whole Church body and affects its ability to function normally.

That is what was happening in Ephesus. The rogue leaders that arose in Paul's absence were like *a bone out of joint,* and there were only two options to deal with them. They could either "pop themselves back into place," submitting to God's authority and getting back in line with correct doctrine, or they could fail to do so and God would remove them. These are the same two options we have today.

Sadly, the Bible tells us these wolfish men had swerved and turned aside from the truth to such a degree that they were engaging in "vain jangling." This is the Greek word *mataiologia,* and it describes *wasted talk; empty words; foolish, nonsensical talk;* or *useless chatter.* Basically, Paul told Timothy that what these misguided leaders were calling "divine revelation" was nothing more than *useless talk* and *wasted words.*

As the head shepherd in Ephesus, Timothy was to command these individuals to "pop themselves back into their place." If they failed to comply, he was to remove them from their places of leadership.

We know from Scripture that many of these "wolves in sheep's clothing" did not repent and realign themselves with truth, and were therefore ousted from their positions of power. In this vacuum of quality overseers, Timothy was faced with the task of filling these places of leadership with men worthy of the position. To help Timothy in his task, Paul gave him several specific qualifications.

The Highest Positions of Church Leadership Are Open to Men *and* Women

In First Timothy 3:1, Paul began by saying, "This is a true saying, If a man desire the office of a bishop, he desireth a good work." The word "true" in this verse is the Greek word *pistos*, and it means *faithful; reliable; dependable;* and *trustworthy*. Hence, Paul was saying, "This is a *faithful, reliable, dependable*, and *trustworthy* saying. What I'm about to tell you, you can totally trust in and lean on to be true."

He then said, "…If a man desire the office of a bishop, he desireth a good work." The words "a man" is a poor translation of the Greek word *tis*, which actually means *anyone — either male or female*. It is not specific to one gender or the other. Interestingly, while there are many denominations that will allow women to teach children and youth, serve as missionaries, and even head up certain departments in the church, they will not permit them to fill the highly visible positions of preaching in the pulpit or pastoring, which is not in agreement with Scripture.

The use of the word *tis* — translated in First Timothy 3:1 as "a man" — throws the door wide open to both men and women serving as a "bishop" in the church. The New Testament reveals that a number of women served in key visible places of leadership in the First Century. Consider Mary Magdalene. John 20:17 records that she was the first person to preach the Gospel after Jesus rose from the grave. History also reveals that she held a position of leadership in the Early Church.

Then there were Philip's four daughters, who are mentioned in Acts 21:9. They stood in the office of the *prophet*, prophesying as the Spirit moved upon them. How about Priscilla? She was the wife of Aquila and is mentioned in Acts 18:2,19, and 26, as well as Romans 16:3 and First Corinthians 16:19. She worked side-by-side with her husband and the apostle Paul, helping to found numerous churches in the First Century, including the church of Corinth and the church of Ephesus.

When we look at Romans 16, we find a record of several women serving in prominent positions in the church. In verse 1, we see a woman named Phebe who served as a *deaconess* in the church of Cenchrea. Moving down to verse 7, we see a woman by the name of Junia, whom Paul said was an *apostle*. Then in verse 15, Paul noted two more women — Julia and the sister of Nereus — who apparently had pastoral responsibilities.

Indeed, the New Testament is replete with examples of women serving in highly visible positions of church leadership. It is no wonder the Holy Spirit moved upon Paul to write Galatians 3:28, which declares, "There is neither Jew nor Greek, there is neither bond nor free, there is *neither male nor female*: for ye are all one in Christ Jesus."

'Desire' Is the Most Important Qualification of a Leader

Of all the qualifications of a leader, the most important is *desire*. Again, Paul wrote, "…If a man desire the office of a bishop, he desireth a good work" (1 Timothy 3:1). The word "desire" is the Greek word *orego*, which means *to stretch forward* or *to reach toward*. It is *the longing, craving, urge, burning desire, or yearning ambition to achieve something or to become something*. This word portrays a person so fixed on the object of his desire that his entire being is stretched forward to take hold of that goal or object.

Basically, Paul said that for a person to become a leader in any capacity in the local church, he or she has to possess a burning desire to fulfill that role, and Paul specifically referred to the "office of a bishop." Again, this phrase "office of a bishop" is the Greek word *episkopos*, and it describes *one who watches, looks, observes, or surveys; one who has oversight or who administrates or manages*. This word indicates a supervisory position and pictures a ruler entrusted with the care of a city or country. It also depicted a political leader who was to provide oversight and management of a region and all the citizens who lived in that region.

Moreover, the word *episkopos* was used to depict construction supervisors who provided oversight of construction sites, ensuring that funds were spent properly, that expenditures didn't exceed the budget, that people did their jobs correctly, and that construction of a building was done in compliance with the desires of the architect. The word also pictures one whose task is to give oversight and who is ultimately responsible for an entire project. Historically, it was used to describe authorized administrative officials in the city of Athens.

The word *episkopos* is where we get the word "bishop." It describes any person in a supervisory, administrative, or managerial position who has oversight. It is such a broad term that it could describe the pastor, a Sunday school teacher, or the janitor of the church. It is anyone responsible for any project or assignment for any department. This doesn't mean he or she does everything. It simply means they are the leader who oversees the project from beginning to the end. Thus according to First Timothy 3:1, the same qualifications God requires of the pastor, He also requires of the janitor. Although there may be different levels of education, talent, or experience required, the basic qualities for a leader (bishop) who serves in any position in God's house are the same.

STUDY QUESTIONS

Study to shew thyself approved unto God, a workman that needeth
not to be ashamed, rightly dividing the word of truth.
— 2 Timothy 2:15

1. It may surprise you to learn that God is not necessarily looking for someone with a Bible school diploma or a seminary degree to serve as a leader. In fact, there are many highly educated people God simply cannot use. Why do you think that is the case? (Consider 1 Corinthians 8:1,2; Isaiah 5:21; and Proverbs 3:7; 26:12.)

2. The corrupt leaders in the church of Ephesus had *ulterior motives*. Specifically, they were trying to draw people away, unto themselves. What leaders come to mind who attempted to build a following for themselves? What eventually became of them? Do you know of any *church leaders* who have fallen into this trap? How about you? Are you trying to build others to *yourself* or to *God*? Ask the Holy Spirit to show you the motives of your heart.

3. Paul said the false teachers that had arisen in the church of Ephesus had so deviated from teaching the truth that they were like *a bone out of joint*. Have you ever dislocated your shoulder, knee, wrist, or some

other joint in your body? How would you describe the pain you experienced? What comparisons can you identify between physical pain and spiritual pain which were talked about in this lesson when a leader is "out of joint"?

PRACTICAL APPLICATION

**But be ye doers of the word, and not hearers only,
deceiving your own selves.
—James 1:22**

1. Prior to this lesson, what was your view regarding women serving in places of Christian leadership? How has your perspective changed after reading the meaning of the words "a man" (the Greek word *tis*) found in First Timothy 3:1?

2. How are you serving as a leader (bishop) at your church? Over what project or group of people are you responsible? How has this lesson impacted your perspective of the responsibilities and position with which you have been entrusted?

LESSON 3

TOPIC

Desire

SCRIPTURES

1. **1 Timothy 3:1,2** — This is a true saying, If a man desire the office of a bishop, he desireth a good work. A bishop then must be blameless, the husband of one wife, vigilant, sober, of good behaviour, given to hospitality, apt to teach.

2. **1 Timothy 5:22** — Lay hands suddenly on no man, neither be partaker of other men's sins: keep thyself pure.

GREEK WORDS

1. "true" — πιστὸς (*pistos*): faithful; reliable; dependable; trustworthy

2. "a man" — **τις** (*tis*): anyone; either male nor female; it is not specific to male or female

3. "desire" — **ὀρέγω** (*orego*): to stretch forward; to reach toward; the longing, craving, urge, burning desire, or yearning ambition to achieve something or to become something; it portrays a person so fixed on the object of his desire that his entire being is stretched forward to take hold of that goal or object

4. "office of a bishop" — **ἐπίσκοπος** (*episkopos*): one who watches, looks, observes, or surveys; one who has oversight or who administrates or manages; a supervisory position; pictures a ruler entrusted with the care of a city or country; depicts a political leader who was to provide oversight and management of a region and of all the citizens who lived in that region; depicts construction supervisors who provided oversight of construction sites, ensuring that funds were spent properly, that expenditures didn't exceed the budget, that people did their jobs correctly, and that construction of a building was done in compliance with the desires of the architect; pictures one whose task is to give oversight and who is ultimately responsible for an entire project from beginning to end; used to describe official administrative officials in the city of Athens; a bishop

5. "good" — **καλός** (*kalos*): beautiful, excellent, good, noble, worthy, honorable, or virtuous; highly esteemed

6. "work" — **ἔργον** (*ergon*): works, deeds, or activity, conveying the idea of work that is produced by consistent and tireless effort

SYNOPSIS

In our previous lessons, we began our journey in the ancient city of Ephesus near the Bouleuterion, which was the place where the city council members gathered regularly to discuss the issues and policies that governed the land. These were not just any men — they were carefully selected, dignified individuals who had a keen ability to think, rationalize, and make important decisions.

Qualified men were not only needed in the civic arena; they were also needed in the Church. In fact, Ephesus was home to the largest church in the region at that time, and after Paul had relinquished his position there and departed, the church experienced a crisis in their leadership. Many who had been serving in high positions of leadership got off into doctrinal error and had to be removed. Timothy, who was serving as the pastor in

Ephesus, needed to know how to choose new leaders to take their place. In response to Timothy's concerns, Paul wrote First Timothy 3, providing a practical list of the qualifications needed to serve in God's house. The number-one requirement to being a leader is *desire*.

The emphasis of this lesson:

To be a leader, you don't need to be talented, highly educated, or have a Bible school degree. Although being theologically educated in the Scriptures is helpful, it is not a requirement to serve in leadership. It is what's inside a man's heart that really counts, and it all starts with *desire*.

Paul Established a Trustworthy Standard for Selecting Leaders

As we learned in our last lesson, Paul began by telling Timothy, "This is a true saying, If a man desire the office of a bishop, he desireth a good work" (1 Timothy 3:1). The word "true" here is the Greek word *pistos*, and it means *faithful, reliable, dependable, and trustworthy*. Using this word was the equivalent of Paul saying, "What I'm about to tell you Timothy is something trustworthy that you can always depend on and rely on."

He then added, "...If a man desire the office of a bishop, he desireth a good work." We saw that the words "a man" is the Greek word *tis*, which means *anyone, either male or female*. Thus the office of a bishop can be filled by both men and women. This shatters the traditional thinking of some denominations and throws the doors open for women to fill key positions of leadership in the Church.

Immediately upon the heels of this revelation, Paul cites the number-one qualification for being a leader. It is *desire*. He said, "...If a man *desire* the office of a bishop, he *desireth* a good work." The word "desire" is the Greek word *orego*, which means *to stretch forward* or *to reach toward*. It describes *a longing, a craving, an urge, a burning desire*, or *a yearning ambition to achieve something or to become something*. It portrays a person so fixed on the object of his desire that his entire being is stretched forward to take hold of that goal or object.

You are never going to advance in life without a desire to do so. You can lack experience and you can lack education, but if you have a burning desire to accomplish something, you have the raw materials needed to become all God planned for you to be!

What Is a Bishop?

Looking again at First Timothy 3:1, Paul said, "…If a man desire the office of a bishop, he desireth a good work." What comes to your mind when you hear the word "bishop"? Many people hear it and automatically see a man dressed in black clothing from head to toe wearing a clerical collar and a gold chain. But that is not what this verse is describing. The word "bishop" here is the Greek word *episkopos*, which is a compound of the word *epi*, meaning *over*, and the word *skopos* meaning *to look*. When the two words are compounded, it basically describes anyone responsible as an overseer.

What is interesting is that the word *episkopos* was a secular word in the First Century and had no religious roots whatsoever. It was used to describe *one who watches, looks, observes, or surveys; one who has oversight or who administrates or manages.* It indicates a supervisory position and pictures a ruler entrusted with the care of a city or country. It can also depict a political leader, such as a mayor or governor, who is to provide oversight and management of a region and of all the citizens who lived in that region.

Moreover, the word *episkopos* was used to depict construction supervisors who provided oversight of construction sites, ensuring that funds were spent properly, that expenditures didn't exceed the budget, that people did their jobs correctly, and that construction of a building was done in compliance with the desires of the architect and local building codes. This word also pictures one whose task is to give oversight and who is ultimately responsible for an entire project from beginning to end.

In First Timothy 3:1, the word *episkopos* is translated as *bishop*. Here it describes any person in a supervisory, administrative, or managerial position in the church who has oversight of other people or a project. The term has such a broad scope that it can describe anyone in church leadership from the lead pastor to a director of ushers and greeters to the church janitor. It is anyone responsible for any project for any department.

Now this doesn't mean he or she does everything. It simply means that person is a leader who oversees an assignment from beginning to the end. Thus the same qualifications God requires of the pastor, He also requires of the janitor. Although each position may require different levels of education, gifting, or experience, the basic qualities for a leader (bishop) who serves in any position in God's house are the same.

Leaders Work Hard and Are Responsible

It is important to notice that the word "desire" actually appears twice in First Timothy 3:1. It says, "…If a man *desire* the office of a bishop, he *desireth* a good work." We have seen that the first appearance of the word "desire" is the Greek word *orego*, which means *to stretch forward* or *to reach toward something with a burning desire to take hold of it.*

The second word "desireth" is the Greek word *epithumia*. It is a compound of the word *epi*, meaning *over*, and the word *thumos*, which depicts *intense passionate desire*. It is *the picture of someone who is passionately and relentlessly in pursuit of something and will stop at nothing to attain it.* This word is so strong, it is often translated as the word "lust." This word "desireth" portrays a growing emotion or yearning that is all-consuming.

Putting these meanings together in the context of this verse, Paul basically said, "If anyone — man or woman — has a burning desire to reach toward being an overseer of people or a project in the church, he or she passionately desires a *good work.*" The word "good" is the Greek word *kalos*, and it describes *something beautiful, excellent, good, honorable, noble, worthy, or virtuous.* And the word "work" is the Greek word *ergon*, which means *works, deeds, or activity* and it conveys *the idea of work that is produced by consistent and tireless effort.*

This lets us know that anyone aspiring to be a leader desires a good thing. However, it will take hard work and sacrifice to see it happen. Being in leadership is a position of responsibility and should not be entered into lightly. That is why Paul also told Timothy *and us*, "Lay hands suddenly on no man, neither be partaker of other men's sins: keep thyself pure" (1 Timothy 5:22). This is a warning not to move too fast when selecting a leader. We need to take time to inspect the person's character. If we mistakenly choose a person without desire, we're going to have a huge problem on our hands.

Just How Important Is Having Desire?

As we noted earlier, you can lack experience and education, but in order to move forward and advance to a place of leadership, having desire is a must.

Have you ever had to work with a *desireless* person? It's like trying to push a 180-ton train engine that is dead on the tracks. You are going nowhere fast. This is why Paul listed desire as the foremost quality every leader should have.

It only takes a few personal experiences with desireless people to understand why Paul made this such an important priority. In his book *Promotion*[1], Rick describes some characteristics of desireless people:

> It's so frustrating when people have the opportunity to learn, to adapt, and to better themselves, but they don't take advantage of these opportunities and therefore never experience needed change. You can send them to school, educate them, even pay for them to fly halfway around the world in order to learn new and better techniques. But if they don't already possess the inner drive to become better and more professional, it doesn't matter how much time or money you throw at them. It's all a waste unless they have *desire*....

> Desireless people stroll through life at their own pace, accepting standards and practices that would *never* be accepted in the business or secular world. As a result, a large portion of the lost world looks at the Church as a pathetic entity made up of a bunch of nincompoops who are not really serious about what they do or say.... Desireless people are like *dead people*! You push, shove, beg, plead, and pray for them to get involved in Kingdom work. Finally, they respond to your constant requests, but they don't do it for long, because they don't have enough desire to be consistent. These people don't have enough desire to make it through obstacles they face along the road in life.

Desire is fundamental to everything else. Desireless people just don't seem to care. Often they appear to be unconcerned. They have no driving motivation to be concerned about anything. Unemotional, they don't have enough passion to feel emotion about what they're doing. They're indifferent. They often have a "take it or leave it" mentality; they're very

---

[1] Renner, Rick. Ten Guidelines To Help You Achieve Your Long-Awaited Promotion! Shippensburg, PA: Harrison House, 2000.

nonchalant. They're of the opinion, *What will be will be, so why try to do anything about it?* Often they're unresponsive; they sit and look at you when you're talking to them as if you haven't even said a word to them.

Very often, they are detached. They're not genuinely connected to any kind of commitment; they are lethargic. They're so lazy, they look like they don't have enough energy to get off the pew or out of their seat. They are inactive. They come to church, but don't ask them to do anything, because they don't have a heart to serve or to be regularly active in anything that requires effort.

Are you beginning to see why the apostle Paul placed desire first in the list of the qualifications for a leader? It would be better to have someone who is uneducated, with little-to-no talent, and full of desire than to have a person with no desire who is highly educated and gifted. The person with desire can grow in knowledge and learn new skills. But the one *without* desire is virtually impossible to motivate or get moving.

Remember, what a person has *in* him is what he's going to impart to all those under his leadership. If he is a person who has desire, he will impart desire to everyone in his department or area of responsibility. However, if he is nonchalant, detached, lethargic, and desireless, that is what he will pass on to those under his care.

A person can only give away what he or she has. The anointing that is on the head will come on the body. The Bible teaches us this in Psalm 133. Hence, a desireless person will create a desireless department.

The truth is, every leader will run into obstacles that try to delay and derail him from achieving his goal. Without desire, that individual will be quickly knocked out of his race and defeated. One has to have a strong desire in order to push through all the difficulties and challenges that will most certainly arise along the way.

In our next lesson, we will focus on the qualification of being *blameless*.

STUDY QUESTIONS

Study to shew thyself approved unto God, a workman that needeth not to be ashamed, rightly dividing the word of truth.
— 2 Timothy 2:15

1. What comes to your mind when you hear the word "bishop"? How have these first three lessons expanded your view of what it means to be a *leader* in the church?

2. Take a few moments to reread the excerpt on desireless people from Rick's book *Promotion*. Are any of these characteristics of lack of desire operating in *your* life? If so, which ones? What do you need to do or change in order stir up a godly desire that propels you forward into God's plan for your life?

3. There are several things noted in Scripture that God encourages us to *desire* and *seek*. Look up these passages and identify these treasures and the reward of obtaining them.

   • Psalm 27:4,8; 42:2; 63:1; and 73:25,26

   • Psalm 119:20,131; 1 Peter 2:2

   • Matthew 5:6

   • 1 Corinthians 12:31; 14:1,12

PRACTICAL APPLICATION

**But be ye doers of the word, and not hearers only,
deceiving your own selves.
—James 1:22**

Take a few moments to sit quietly and honestly ask yourself these soul-searching questions:

1. *Am I nonchalant about life, or do I truly have the desire to do what's right and to be all God has called me to be?*

2. *In what specific ways is my life demonstrating healthy desire? In what areas is it strongest?*

3. *How am I preparing and bettering myself to serve as a leader in God's house and in life?*

If you lack desire, there is no need to feel bad about yourself. Simply pray and ask the Holy Spirit to ignite a fire of healthy desire for the things He wants you to do. All He asks of you is that you have an open, willing heart.

TOPIC
Blameless

SCRIPTURES

1. **1 Timothy 3:1,2** — This is a true saying, If a man desire the office of a bishop, he desireth a good work. A bishop then must be blameless, the husband of one wife, vigilant, sober, of good behaviour, given to hospitality, apt to teach.

GREEK WORDS

1. "true" — **πιστὸς** (*pistos*): faithful; reliable; dependable; trustworthy

2. "a man" — **τις** (*tis*): anyone; either male or female; it is not specific to male or female

3. "desire" — **ὀρέγω** (*orego*): to stretch forward; to reach toward; the longing, craving, urge, burning desire, or yearning ambition to achieve something or to become something; it portrays a person so fixed on the object of his desire that his entire being is stretched forward to take hold of that goal or object

4. "office of a bishop" — **ἐπίσκοπος** (*episkopos*): one who watches, looks, observes, or surveys; one who has oversight or who administrates or manages; a supervisory position; pictures a ruler entrusted with the care of a city or country; depicts a political leader who was to provide oversight and management of a region and of all the citizens who lived in that region; depicts construction supervisors who provided oversight of construction sites, ensuring that funds were spent properly, that expenditures didn't exceed the budget, that people did their jobs correctly, and that construction of a building was done in compliance with the desires of the architect; pictures one whose task is to give oversight and who is ultimately responsible for an entire project from beginning to end; used to describe official administrative officials in the city of Athens; a bishop

5. "good" — **καλός** (*kalos*): beautiful, excellent, good, noble, worthy, honorable, or virtuous; highly esteemed

6. "work" — ἔργον (*ergon*): works, deeds, or activity, conveying the idea of work that is produced by consistent and tireless effort

7. "bishop" — ἐπίσκοπος (*episkopos*): one who watches, looks, observes, or surveys; one who has oversight or who administrates or manages; pictures a supervisory position

8. "then" — οὖν (*oun*): therefore; consequently; accordingly

9. "must be" — δεῖ (*dei*): an obligation or necessity; absolutely must be

10. "blameless" — ἀνεπίληπτος (*anepilemptos*): denotes one whose reputation has been restored, regardless of how reproachful or shameful that person's actions once were; former blame has been removed and now this individual is blameless; in spite of a lurid past, there is now nothing to disqualify this person because blame is removed, and he has become blame-free; pictures one who has no obvious flaws that would be a stumbling block to people and hinder them from following him; one with no blatant outward flaws

SYNOPSIS

The rich, regal city of Ephesus was not the only city in the First Century to have a Bouleuterion. The fact is, nearly every large city in ancient times had one. The word Bouleuterion comes from the word *boules*, which means *to counsel*. The Bouleuterions in these cities were the place where the members of the city council regularly met to hear the issues the people were facing, to decide public policies, and to make crucial decisions. The individuals who served on this council had a blameless reputation. In the same way, God calls those who serve as leaders in the Church to live a blameless life.

We learned in the first lesson that *desire* is the first qualification for spiritual leadership in the local church according to First Timothy 3:1. *Blamelessness* is the second qualification of a good leader given to us by Paul in this passage. When you hear the word "blameless," you may think, *Well, that disqualifies me. I'm not perfect, and I'll never be perfect.* But being blameless does not mean being perfect, as we will see in the lesson.

The emphasis of this lesson:

Being blameless is the second qualification of a good leader. Contrary to what you may think, being blameless doesn't mean being perfect. Only Jesus was perfect, and only He can make a person blameless.

What We've Learned So Far
A Review of First Timothy 3:1

As we learned in our first lesson, the apostle Paul told the elders at the church of Ephesus that after he had departed, spiritual wolves would arise from among their number that had no regard for the wellbeing of the people. They would twist the Gospel message for their own gain in an attempt to gather disciples unto themselves (*see* Acts 20:29,30).

Sure enough, what Paul predicted came to pass. This left Timothy, the young pastor of the church, with the task of removing the corrupt leaders and replacing them with new ones. To help him select the best leaders, Paul gave him a list of qualifications each individual should have. He began by saying, "This is a true saying, If a man desire the office of a bishop, he desireth a good work" (1 Timothy 3:1).

We have seen that the word **"true"** in this verse is the Greek word *pistos*, and it means *faithful, reliable, dependable*, and *trustworthy*. By using this word, it was the equivalent of Paul saying, "What I'm about to tell you is a *faithful, reliable, dependable*, and *trustworthy* saying. You can totally depend on it to be true."

Next, we learned the definition of the words **"a man,"** which is the Greek word *tis*, meaning *anyone — either male or female*. This word *tis* is not specific to either gender. Biblically, this throws the doors wide open to anyone — man or woman — who has a "desire" to serve in any area of church leadership.

The word **"desire"** in this verse is the Greek word *orego*, which means *to stretch forward* or *to reach toward something*. It depicts *a longing, a craving, an urge, a burning desire or yearning ambition to achieve something or to become something*. It portrays a person so fixed on the object of his desire that his entire being is stretched forward to take hold of that goal or object. Desire is the foundational characteristic a person needs to be a leader. A person with desire — even if he or she lacks education and talent — has great potential to become a great leader.

This brings us to the phrase **"office of a bishop."** What is interesting is that in the Greek, the word "office" does not appear. It simply says, "If anyone desires to be a bishop." The word "bishop" is the Greek word *episkopos*, which is a compound of the word *epi*, meaning *over*, and the word *skopos*, meaning *to look*. The word *skopos* is where we derive the words "microscope" and "telescope."

When the words *epi* and *skopos* are compounded to form *episkopos*, it describes *one who watches, looks, observes, or surveys; one who has oversight or who administrates or manages*. In Ancient Greek culture, it *pictured a ruler entrusted with the care of a city or country*. It also pictured *a political leader who was to provide oversight and management of a region and of all the citizens who lived in that region*.

Furthermore, the word *episkopos* — translated here as "bishop" — has been used to depict a construction supervisor who provided oversight of construction sites, ensuring that funds were spent properly, that expenditures didn't exceed the budget, that people did their jobs correctly, and that construction of a building was done in compliance with the desires of the architect and city codes. In essence, a "bishop" (*episkopos*) is *one who has ultimate responsibility for people or projects*. Thus a "bishop" can be any person serving in the church — from the lead pastor to a Sunday school teacher to the church janitor. This means the same qualifications God requires of a pastor, He also requires of the church janitor.

The Bible goes on to state that anyone who desires to have a supervisory, leadership position in the church, "...desireth a good work" (1 Timothy 3:1). We saw in our last lesson that the word **"good"** is the Greek word *kalos*, and it describes *something beautiful, excellent, good, honorable, noble, worthy*, or *virtuous*. And the word **"work"** is the Greek word *ergon*, which conveys *the idea of work that is produced by consistent and tireless effort*. So while desiring to be a leader of people or projects is an honorable ambition, you must keep in mind it will require hard work and sacrifice to bring it about.

What It Means To Be 'Blameless'

Paul also wrote that in addition to a person having *desire*, "A bishop then must be *blameless*, the husband of one wife, vigilant, sober, of good behaviour, given to hospitality, apt to teach" (1 Timothy 3:2). Here again, we see the word "bishop," which is the same Greek word *episkopos*, describing *one who watches, looks, observes, or surveys; one who has oversight or who administrates or manages*. It pictures a leader in God's house in a supervisory position who oversees a project or a group of people.

The Scripture says, "A bishop then must be blameless...." But even the word "then" is important here. In Greek, it is the word *oun*, and it means *therefore, consequently*, or *accordingly*. The phrase "must be" is a translation of the Greek word *dei*, which indicates *an obligation or necessity; something that absolutely and emphatically must be*. The use of this word leaves no room for exceptions. A "bishop" — or church leader — absolutely, positively must be "blameless."

Many people desire to be a leader until they hear that a leader must be "blameless." They erroneously believe that "blameless" means perfect, and that is not the case. There is no such thing as a perfect leader. Only one leader on earth was perfect and that was Jesus. The word "blameless" here is the Greek word *anepilemptos*, which is a compound of three words: *a*, *epi*, and *lemptos*, which is a form of the Greek word *lambano*. The word *epi* means *against*, and the root word *lambano* means *to receive* or *to grab hold of*. These two words combined by themselves indicate there is something in a person's character that is so corrupt you could grab hold of it and use it against them. However, when an "a" is placed in front of this word, it has a canceling effect that gives it the *opposite* meaning.

Hence, the word for "blameless" — *anepilemptos* — describes *a person who once acted shamefully*. Yet, regardless of how reproachful or shameful his or her actions once were, this word denotes that *their reputation has been restored*. Their former blame has been removed, and now this individual is *blameless*. In spite of a lurid past, there is now nothing to disqualify this person because blame is removed, and he has become blame-free. It is a picture of *one who has no obvious flaws that would be a stumbling block to people that would hinder them from following him or her* or *one with no blatant outward flaws*.

The reality is, everyone has flaws in his or her life. Romans 3:23 says, "For all have sinned, and come short of the glory of God." Nevertheless, through faith in the redemptive work of Jesus Christ — the belief that He was and is the sinless Son of God who died in our place and was raised back to life — our flaws can be forgiven! They can be erased and forever removed from our lives (*see* Psalm 103:12). And by His grace, we can rise above the life we once lived and begin living holy lives.

Thus being blameless means you no longer have any area in your life that is so blatantly wrong that someone can grab hold of it (*epilambano*) and claim it as a reason against you not to follow you as a leader. In other words, there is nothing blatantly wrong in your life that would cause people to stumble in their walk with God.

Leaders Must Be Free of Blatant Sin

Essentially, the Holy Spirit spoke through Paul and said, "When you choose a leader, choose a person who has a burning desire to be a leader, and at the same time, select someone who doesn't have obvious, blatant defects in his or her character that would hinder people from following Christ and from following that leader's example.

A person who has blatant sin operating in his life is one who has lost his authority to speak into the lives of others. Regardless of the level of leadership in which you are operating, there are people around you watching your life. The witness of your life has to back up the message from your mouth. Your actions are on display, and if you have any obvious flaw in your life, it will be something a person can grab hold of as a reason not to follow you and ultimately, not to follow Christ.

Friend, if you have an area in your life that is out of order — a glaring defect that others can grab hold of and hold against you — that does not necessarily eliminate you from being a leader in God's house. Just sincerely confess and repent of any sin (*see* 1 John 1:9), receive God's forgiveness and the power of His Holy Spirit, and take the necessary steps to deal with the defects in your life.

In our next lesson, we will examine what it means to be *"the husband of one wife."*

STUDY QUESTIONS

**Study to shew thyself approved unto God, a workman that needeth not to be ashamed, rightly dividing the word of truth.
— 2 Timothy 2:15**

As a child of God, you are a new creation (*see* 2 Corinthians 5:17). When God looks at you, He sees you as *blameless* and *righteous* in Christ Jesus (*see* 2 Corinthians 5:21). If you are feeling condemned, you can know with certainty it is not God speaking to you. Take time to chew on these powerful truths from Scripture and write what the Holy Spirit speaks to you.

1. **Romans 8:1,2**
2. **Romans 8:31-39**
3. **John 3:17,18**
4. **1 John 3:19,20**

PRACTICAL APPLICATION

But be ye doers of the word, and not hearers only,
deceiving your own selves.
—James 1:22

1. Briefly describe the difference between being *blameless* and being *perfect*. How does understanding the meaning of being blameless encourage you? Do you know someone who desperately needs to hear this truth?

2. Can you think of an area in your life that would hinder others from following you as a leader? If so, what are they? What action steps do you sense the Holy Spirit is asking you to take to make things right and remove any cause for stumbling (*see* Romans 14:13,19; 1 Corinthians 8:9)?

3. If you have an area in your life that is out of order — a glaring defect others can grab hold of and hold against you — take time now to confess and repent of it (*see* 1 John1:9). Receive God's forgiveness and the power of His Holy Spirit and begin walking in newness of life (*see* Romans 6:3-5).

LESSON 5

TOPIC

The Husband of One Wife

SCRIPTURES

1. **1 Timothy 3:1,2** — This is a true saying, If a man desire the office of a bishop, he desireth a good work. A bishop then must be blameless, the husband of one wife, vigilant, sober, of good behaviour, given to hospitality, apt to teach.

2. **2 Corinthians 5:17** — Therefore if any man be in Christ, he is a new creature: old things are passed away; behold, all things are become new.

GREEK WORDS

1. "true" — πιστὸς (*pistos*): faithful; reliable; dependable; trustworthy

2. "a man" — τις (*tis*): anyone; either male or female; it is not specific to male or female

3. "desire" — ὀρέγω (*orego*): to stretch forward; to reach toward; the longing, craving, urge, burning desire, or yearning ambition to achieve something or to become something; it portrays a person so fixed on the object of his desire that his entire being is stretched forward to take hold of that goal or object

4. "office of a bishop" — ἐπίσκοπος (*episkopos*): one who watches, looks, observes, or surveys; one who has oversight or who administrates or manages; a supervisory position; pictures a ruler entrusted with the care of a city or country; depicts a political leader who was to provide oversight and management of a region and of all the citizens who lived in that region; depicts construction supervisors who provided oversight of construction sites, ensuring that funds were spent properly, that expenditures didn't exceed the budget, that people did their jobs correctly, and that construction of a building was done in compliance with the desires of the architect; pictures one whose task is to give oversight and who is ultimately responsible for an entire project from beginning to end; used to describe official administrative officials in the city of Athens; a bishop

5. "good" — καλός (*kalos*): beautiful, excellent, good, noble, worthy, honorable, or virtuous; highly esteemed

6. "work" — ἔργον (*ergon*): works, deeds, or activity, conveying the idea of work that is produced by consistent and tireless effort

7. "then" — οὖν (*oun*): therefore; consequently; accordingly

8. "must be" — δεῖ (*dei*): an obligation or necessity; absolutely must be

9. "blameless" — ἀνεπίληπτος (*anepilemptos*): denotes one whose reputation has been restored, regardless of how reproachful or shameful that person's actions once were; former blame has been removed and now this individual is blameless; in spite of a lurid past, there is now nothing to disqualify this person because blame is removed, and he has become blame-free; pictures one who has no obvious flaws that

would be a stumbling block to people and hinder them from following him; one with no blatant outward flaws

10. "the husband of one wife" — **μιᾶς γυναικὸς ἄνδρα** (*mias gunaikos andra*): literally, a one-woman man; a one-woman sort of man; a man who has fidelity to one woman if he is married

SYNOPSIS

When we look at the Bouleuterion in the ancient city of Ephesus, we see a place where dignified magistrates, dressed in royal robes, sat together to discuss, debate, and decide public policies and moral issues. These highly qualified men of character were chosen to be the town fathers and to serve as guides for the city.

In the same way, highly qualified individuals were needed to serve as spiritual leaders within the church of Ephesus. In the First Century, it was the largest church in the world, and as such, it was home to some of the biggest church problems the world had ever seen. Doctrinal error had crept into the congregation, causing many seasoned leaders to become self-seeking and perverted in their thinking and teaching.

At that time, Timothy was the pastor of the church, and he had the arduous task of uprooting the corrupt leaders and choosing new, qualified leaders to replace them. He wrote to Paul, his mentor, and asked him for guidance. Paul wrote back and in First Timothy 3 gave Timothy — *and us* — a practical list of qualifications needed for leadership in the house of God.

The emphasis of this lesson:

The third qualification for a leader in the church is that he must be "the husband of one wife." This does not mean that a leader must be married or never have been divorced; it does mean a leader must show integrity in his or her relationships.

A Brief Review
First Timothy 3:1

The apostle Paul began by saying:

This is a true saying, If a man desire the office of a bishop, he desireth a good work.

> **— 1 Timothy 3:1**

The word **"true"** here is the Greek word *pistos*, meaning *faithful*; *reliable*; *dependable*; and *trustworthy*. The guidelines Paul gave Timothy for choosing leaders were that they must be *faithful*; *reliable*; *dependable*; and *trustworthy*.

The phrase **"a man"** is the Greek word *tis*, and it describes *anyone — either male or female*; it is gender neutral. Hence, Paul opened the doors for any man or woman who met the qualifications to serve as a leader in the Church. Clearly, he had no issues with female leaders. One look at New Testament writings reveals he had a plethora of women who served alongside him in ministry.

The word **"desire"** is the Greek word *orego*, which means *to stretch forward* or *to reach toward*. It is *a longing, a craving, an urge, a burning desire, or a yearning ambition to achieve something or to become something*. "Desire" is the first and foremost qualification of being a leader. In order to grow as a leader, desire is *required*. Likewise, because of the "intestinal fortitude" it produces, desire is also needed to confront and conquer the inevitable obstacles you will face along the way. So before signing up to be a leader, make sure you have the necessary *desire* for leadership. And before you place someone in a leadership position, make sure he or she has the desire necessary to fulfill that role.

The phrase **"office of a bishop"** is the Greek word *episkopos*, which would be better translated as *an overseer* as it is in Acts 20:28. This word describes *one who watches, looks, observes, or surveys; one who has oversight or who administrates or manages*. It depicts a supervisory position, such as a ruler in history who was entrusted with the care of a city or country or a political leader who was to provide oversight and management of a region and of all the citizens who lived in that region. This very word was used to describe administrators who superintended the city of Athens.

Keep in mind that when the New Testament was written, the emerging Church did not have its own vocabulary. Thus the majority of the words used in Scripture were borrowed from the secular world. The word *episkopos* — translated here as "bishop" — is a perfect example. This word was often used to depict construction supervisors who provided oversight of construction sites, ensuring that funds were spent properly, expenditures didn't exceed the budget, people did their jobs correctly, and the construction of a building was done in compliance with the desires of the architect. Paul's use of this word was strategic; it was the equivalent of his telling Timothy to choose leaders who would help him *oversee the building* of the Church.

Essentially, the word *episkopos* describes *anyone with responsibility and oversight for people or projects*. It pictures one whose task is to give oversight and who is ultimately responsible for an entire project from beginning to end. Hence, within the realm of the church, the word "bishop" could describe the pastor, the worship leader, the children's church teacher, the head deacon, or the church janitor.

The Bible goes on to say that the one who desires to be a bishop in the church desires a **"good work."** The word **"good"** is the Greek word *kalos*, which describes *something beautiful, excellent, good, honorable, noble, worthy, or virtuous*. And the word **"work"** is the Greek word *ergon*, which describes *works, deeds, or activity*; it conveys the idea of *work that is produced by consistent and tireless effort*. This indicates that when you're serving as a leader in ministry, it often includes sleepless nights and unending effort.

A Leader Must Be 'Blameless'

In First Timothy 3:2, the apostle Paul added to the list of leadership qualifications. He continued, "A bishop then must be blameless, the husband of one wife, vigilant, sober, of good behaviour, given to hospitality, apt to teach." Here again, we see the word "bishop" — the Greek word *episkopos* — which describes *an overseer* or *a visible leader who watches, looks, observes, or surveys; one who has oversight or who administrates or manages*.

The Bible says, "A bishop *then* must be blameless...." Before we get to the word "blameless," it's important to note that even the word "then" has significance. It is the Greek word *oun*, which means *therefore, consequently, or accordingly*. And the phrase "must be" is the Greek word *dei*, and it describes *an obligation or necessity; something that absolutely must be*. The inclusion of these words — "then must be" — emphatically indicates there is absolutely no room for questioning. A bishop absolutely, positively *must be* blameless.

In our last lesson, we learned that the word "blameless" in Greek is the word *anepilemptos*. It describes *one who once had a reproachful background, but now that person's reputation has been completely restored*. In fact, this word denotes that regardless of how dreadful or shameful a person's actions once were, his reputation has been restored. All former blame has been removed and now this individual is blameless. In spite of a lurid past, there is now nothing to disqualify him from being a leader because blame has been removed, and he has become blame-free. It is a picture of *one who has no obvious flaws that would be a stumbling block to people and hinder them from following him.*

Basically, Paul told Timothy — *and us* — to make sure that when we choose leaders, we select people who have a good reputation. Even if they had a bad reputation in the past, make sure that they are now blame-free, living a life submitted in obedience to the Word of God, changed and displaying a godly life. In this condition, they are in a position to be a viable leader in the church.

A Leader Must Be 'the Husband of One Wife'

Immediately after telling Timothy a bishop needs to be blameless, Paul added the requirement "the husband of one wife." Among Scripture verses that have been misunderstood by believers, this is certainly one of them. In the original Greek text, this phrase "the husband of one wife" literally says *a one-woman man; a one-woman sort of man; or a man who has fidelity to one woman if he is married.*

Some denominations have mistakenly taught that the words "the husband of one wife" mean a man in church leadership can never be divorced. For instance, in the former USSR, there are many who believe and teach that this phrase means a man cannot serve as a leader in the church if he is divorced and remarried or even if his wife died and he remarried. In both cases, they argue that this man would have had two wives, which they believe contradicts this scripture. Still others believe and teach that "the husband of one wife" means a leader in the church *has* to be married. Neither of those beliefs is necessarily true.

So what does 'the husband of one wife' really mean?

First of all, the phrase "the husband of one wife" is a *present-tense* statement. Thus it implies that a man serving as a church leader should be currently married to only one woman. It was a warning against polygamy, not remarriage after a divorce or the death of a spouse.

A careful look at the New Testament Roman world reveals that society was riddled with divorce and sexual impurity. In fact, the church at Ephesus was primarily a Gentile church, and it was filled with people who had come out of fornication, adultery, abuse, and relational brokenness of all kinds. This was the church Timothy was pastoring when Paul wrote the qualifications of leadership in First Timothy 3. Think about it: — Finding a sizeable group of leaders who were married only once would have been a huge challenge.

Moreover, many people in the First Century who came to Christ had formerly been fornicators, adulterers, and homosexuals. Others were previously thieves and even murderers. However, once they were forgiven and cleansed by the blood of Jesus, these individuals became candidates to serve as leaders in the church. So why was it okay for people with these types of sins to serve as leaders, but not those broken by divorce? Does the blood of Jesus not restore all these forms of deviancy *as well as* the brokenness of divorce? The answer is *yes*, it does!

The truth is, the words "the husband of one wife" refer to a man who is known for being faithfully committed to his wife in the present tense. That is, he is not a polygamist. If his wife died and he married a second time, he is eligible to serve in leadership. Likewise, if he got divorced before he surrendered to Christ, he is eligible to serve in leadership.

What about those who are single? Are the words 'the husband of one wife' a mandate to be married?

Absolutely not. Most scholars agree that the words "the husband of one wife" do *not* mean that a spiritual leader *must* be married. The apostle Paul was not married. Neither was Timothy, Barnabas, or the apostle John. In fact, Jesus was also single! If being married was a requirement for serving in church leadership, all of these men would have been disqualified.

What if a leader's spouse dies and that leader remarries? Is he disqualified from staying in leadership?

No. If this was the case, then if a leader's spouse died, his ministry would die also. How can we look into the face of a man who has just lost his wife and tell him he can no longer minister after he has faithfully served God's people? Where is the love and compassion in that? This makes no sense, and there is no biblical basis to support such a belief.

What about someone who got divorced *after* coming to Christ? Can he or she be a leader?

The truth is, we live in a world that is filled with brokenness, and Christians sometimes end up getting divorced for various reasons. Many did not want a divorce, and it was not their fault. In cases like these, it is best to leave judgment in the hands of God who sees all the details clearly. Let your pastor and spiritual leaders handle these situations and pray for them to hear and have the heart of God on the matter.

The Bottom Line Is *This*

If a man is married, he must be faithfully committed to his present wife — meaning, he's working on his marriage and is an example to others of integrity and fidelity. It doesn't matter what happened in his life previously. He may have been divorced, unfaithful, a thief, or a murderer — all of that was *before* Christ. If he is saved and in Christ, his reputation can be fully restored. Walking out his new life in Christ, he is now blame-free and qualified to serve as a leader in the church.

Through Paul, the Holy Spirit penned this powerful word of hope: "Therefore if any man be in Christ, he is a new creature: old things are passed away; behold, all things are become new" (2 Corinthians 5:17). This verse tells us when a person comes to Christ, his or her slate is totally wiped clean. It's as if the "clock" for that individual's life has been reset and time starts ticking all over again.

God does not hold a person's old life against his new life in Christ, and neither should we! Those who are born again are new creatures in Him! If we held people hostage because of what they did before they came to Christ, no one would ever qualify to be used by God.

Again, in the original Greek, Paul's words declaring that a leader must be "the husband of one wife" literally states that he must be *a one-woman man; a one-woman sort of man; or a man who has fidelity to one woman if he is married.* This portion of Scripture is actually dealing with the issue of *commitment.* You don't want to choose people to be leaders who don't have commitment to their spouse and family. If they're not committed to their family, they won't be *truly* committed to anyone else.

STUDY QUESTIONS

Study to shew thyself approved unto God, a workman that
needeth not to be ashamed, rightly dividing the word of truth.
— 2 Timothy 2:15

1. Before this lesson, had you ever heard this verse that says, "A bishop then must be...the husband of one wife..." (1 Timothy 3:2)? If you had heard it, what did you understand it to mean? How has this lesson clarified your understanding of this part of the passage?

2. As you know, not every situation has a clear, defined, "right" answer. Some things just aren't black-and-white. Is there someone in your life you've been tempted to judge or write off just because he has been divorced, or because he has had some other relationship issue? Read First Corinthians 4:5. Does it cause you to rethink your conclusion? If so, how?

PRACTICAL APPLICATION

But be ye doers of the word, and not hearers only,
deceiving your own selves.
— James 1:22

1. Who do you know in your church who has gone through divorce and has since been banned from the pulpit or forbidden in ministry? How can you take what you learned in this teaching to offer hope and encouragement to this saint?

2. After going through this teaching, how would you respond to someone who has misunderstood this passage and is trying to prevent someone else from serving in ministry on the basis of divorce or former sin?

TOPIC

Vigilant, Sober, Good Behavior, Hospitality, Apt To Teach

SCRIPTURES

1. **1 Timothy 3:1,2** — This is a true saying, If a man desire the office of a bishop, he desireth a good work. A bishop then must be blameless, the husband of one wife, vigilant, sober, of good behaviour, given to hospitality, apt to teach.

GREEK WORDS

1. "true" — **πιστὸς** (*pistos*): faithful; reliable; dependable; trustworthy

2. "a man" — **τις** (*tis*): anyone; either male nor female; it is not specific to male or female

3. "desire" — **ὀρέγω** (*orego*): to stretch forward; to reach toward; the longing, craving, urge, burning desire, or yearning ambition to achieve something or to become something; it portrays a person so fixed on the object of his desire that his entire being is stretched forward to take hold of that goal or object

4. "bishop" — **ἐπίσκοπος** (*episkopos*): one who watches, looks, observes, or surveys; one who has oversight or who administrates or manages; a supervisory position; a visible leader

5. "good" — **καλός** (*kalos*): beautiful, excellent, good, noble, worthy, honorable, or virtuous; highly esteemed

6. "work" — **ἔργον** (*ergon*): works, deeds, or activity, conveying the idea of work that is produced by consistent and tireless effort

7. "then" — **οὖν** (*oun*): therefore; consequently; accordingly

8. "must be" — **δεῖ** (*dei*): an obligation or necessity; absolutely must be

9. "blameless" — **ἀνεπίληπτος** (*anepilemptos*): denotes one whose reputation has been restored regardless of how reproachful or shameful his or her actions once were; former blame has been removed and now this individual is blameless; in spite of a lurid past, there is now nothing to disqualify this person because blame is removed, and he has

become blame-free; pictures one who has no obvious flaws that would be a stumbling block to people to hinder them from following him or her; one with no blatant, outward flaws

10. "the husband of one wife" — **μιᾶς γυναικὸς ἄνδρα** (*mias gunaikos andra*): literally a one-woman man; a one-woman sort of man; a man who has the character of fidelity to one woman if he is married

11. "vigilant" — **νηφαλέος** (*nephalios*): sober, not like a silly drunk; not intoxicated with silliness; serious-minded

12. "sober" — **σωφρονέω** (*sophroneo*): to be of sound mind; reasonable; balanced; levelheaded in the way one thinks

13. "good behavior" — **κόσμιος** (*kosmios*): from **κόσμος** (*kosmos*); depicts something that is ordered; it is where we get the words "cosmos" and "cosmetics"; when it becomes **κόσμιος** (*kosmios*), it pictures one whose life is in order; applies to every sphere of one's existence — relationships, finances, property, etc.

14. "given to hospitality" — **φιλόξενος** (*philoxenos*): love for a foreigner or stranger; having an open-home mentality

15. "apt to teach" — **διδακτικός** (*didaktikos*): pictures one who is skillful in teaching; a communicator

SYNOPSIS

As we have seen, the Bouleuterion in the upper region of ancient Ephesus was the gathering place of an elite group of men who served as the city councilors. They came together on a regular basis to deal with the issues, hammer out the details of public policies, and make decisions for the citizens of Ephesus. These were the *episkopos* of the city — the supervisors and administrators who managed the city's affairs.

The word *episkopos* is the same term used by Paul to describe one who served as a "bishop," or leader, in the church. He lists the qualifications for leadership in First Timothy 3. Thus far, we have seen that having *desire*, being *blameless*, and being *the husband of one wife* are all attributes leaders must possess. Paul went on to declare that leaders must also be "…vigilant, sober, of good behaviour, given to hospitality, apt to teach" (1 Timothy 3:2).

The emphasis of this lesson:

As leaders in God's house, we are to be serious-minded, sober, and levelheaded in our thinking; we are to have a generous, "open-home" mentality, and take every opportunity to use our personal lives to teach others.

A Review of Our Anchor Verse

Having been appointed by Paul to be the pastor of the church of Ephesus, Timothy was charged with the duty of uprooting rebellious leaders and replacing them with qualified men of integrity. Seeking godly counsel, he wrote to Paul, and Paul responded with a list of practical requirements for anyone who wanted to serve in God's house. First Timothy 3:1 says, "This is a true saying, If a man desire the office of a bishop, he desireth a good work." Here is a quick review of the key words in this verse:

> **"True"** is the Greek word *pistos*, which means *faithful; reliable; dependable; trustworthy*.

> **"A man"** in Greek is the word *tis*, and it describes *anyone; either male or female*. It is *not specific to male or female*. This throws the door open for anyone to serve as a leader in God's house.

> **"Desire"** is the Greek word *orego*, which means *to stretch forward; to reach toward*. It is *a longing, a craving, an urge, a burning desire, or yearning ambition to achieve something or to become something;* it portrays *a person so fixed on the object of his desire that his entire being is stretched forward to take hold of that goal or object*. When a person with desire is in a position of authority, he will stir up desire in all those serving under him. Desire is the foundational qualification to being a leader.

Paul said, "…If a man desire the office of a bishop, he desireth a good work" (1 Timothy 3:1). Interestingly, the word "office" does not appear in the original Greek. It simply says "bishop," which is the Greek word *episkopos*, a compound of the words *epi* and *skopos*. The word *epi* means *over*, and the word *skopos* means *to look*. When these words are compounded to form the word *episkopos*, it denotes *one who has oversight over people or over projects*. Basically, *episkopos* describes *a visible leader*.

Anyone — man or woman — who desires to be a visible leader in God's house desires a "good work." We saw that the word "good" is the Greek word *kalos*, which describes *something beautiful, excellent, good, honorable, noble, worthy, or virtuous*. And the word "work" in Greek is the word *ergon*, which indicates *works, deeds, or activity,* and it conveys *the idea of work that is produced by consistent and tireless effort.* Thus, leadership is not just about a grandiose title, a big office, and a large group of people to direct. Leadership is about hard work and focused effort with the purpose of advancing God's Kingdom.

Leaders Are To Be 'Vigilant, Sober, and of Good Behavior'

In First Timothy 3:2, Paul added, "A bishop then must be blameless, the husband of one wife, vigilant, sober, of good behaviour...." In Lesson 4, we focused on the meaning of the word "blameless," and in Lesson 5, we examined what the Bible means to be "the husband of one wife." Please refer back to those lessons to refresh your understanding of these characteristics.

The next qualification of leadership is vigilance. The word "vigilant" in this verse is the Greek word *nephalios*, and it means *sober, not like a silly drunk; not intoxicated with silliness; serious-minded.* The use of this word is the equivalent of Paul telling Timothy, "Make sure you only put those in leadership who understand the seriousness of the office." Although it is not wrong to have fun at times, serving in a position of authority is one of the most important callings on the planet. People's lives are at stake and in need of healing.

Along with being "vigilant," the Bible says leaders are to be "sober," which is the Greek word *sophroneo*, and it means *to be of sound mind; to be reasonable; balanced; levelheaded in the way one thinks.* Moreover, Paul said leaders should exhibit "good behavior." This is the Greek word *kosmios*, which is from the word *kosmos*, and it depicts *something that is ordered.* It is where we get the word "cosmos," which describes *the orderliness of the universe.* The word "cosmetics" is also derived from *kosmos*, which indicates that when a woman uses cosmetics, she brings order to her face. When *kosmos* becomes the word *kosmios* — translated here as "good behavior" — it pictures *one whose life is in order,* and it applies to every sphere of one's existence, including relationships, finances, property, etc.

Leaders Are People 'Given to Hospitality'

Next the Bible says, "A bishop then must be...given to hospitality..." (1 Timothy 3:2). This phrase is a compound of the word *philos*, which means *to love*, and the word *xenos*, which is the word for *a stranger*. When the two words are fused together to form the word *philoxenos*, it describes *love for a foreigner or stranger; having an open-home mentality.* This attribute was very important during the First Century as many Christians suffered persecution and lost their homes because of their faith in Christ. When this occurred, godly leaders would open their homes and care for the people until they found a place to live.

Today, having an open-home mentality is still very important. It says to the Lord, and to others, that we want to use our most valuable resources to be a blessing to God's people. If a leader says that his home is off-limits, it is a signal that he will have limitations to his commitment and how far he is willing to go in his service to others.

Leaders Are 'Apt To Teach'

Finally, Paul told Timothy that those in visible leadership should be "apt to teach." While this may seem to suggest that a leader must be highly educated and know the New Testament Greek and the Old Testament Hebrew, it is not the case. The phrase "apt to teach" is the Greek word *didaktikos*, and it pictures *one who is skillful in teaching* or *a communicator.*

The fact is, leadership is all about communication. Whether a leader realizes it or not, he or she is communicating to others all the time — most often without words. For instance, when it is time to worship, people are watching those in leadership to see how they are responding. Are their hands raised or in their pockets? Are they singing from their hearts or scrolling on their phone? Their actions are communicating.

Likewise, how a leader treats his or her spouse and children is speaking volumes to onlookers. Are these leaders loving and attentive or harsh and neglectful? Similarly, when it comes time to give in the offering, are they participating or are they disengaged? In all situations and in every environment, people are watching. Each action and reaction is a message being communicated. Contrary to what some people have said, our private life *does* affect our public influence. Indeed, our personal life is our most powerful pulpit.

The Trickle-Down Effect Is Always at Work

Keep in mind the principle found in Psalm 133:2, which talks about the anointing of blessing that flowed down Aaron the priest's beard. *Whatever is on the head, will come upon the entire body.* If a person steeped in silliness is chosen to lead others, silliness will come upon everyone under his leadership. Likewise, a person who is out of balance and extreme in his or her views will impart the same type of character to those he or she leads. The same holds true for people who are inhospitable and unloving to strangers as well as for those who live a life of constant disorder. The negative behavior the leader exhibits will negatively influence others to act in the same manner.

Thankfully, the opposite is also true. If a vigilant, serious-minded person is chosen to be a leader, he will impart a vigilant, serious-minded perspective to those he leads. If a leader is sober, levelheaded, and balanced, he will produce like qualities in those he oversees. If he exhibits good behavior and lives an orderly life, he will influence the people under his authority to mirror his actions. Likewise, if he is given to hospitality and apt to teach, he will inspire others to do the same. Indeed, what a person has in him is inevitably what he is going to give to others.

Friend, if you see any area of your life where you need to come up higher in how you are living, simply repent and take the steps necessary to self-correct. Don't come under condemnation and judgment — that will not help you or change anything. Just say, "Lord, forgive me. This is an area where I need to improve." As you humble yourself before God, He will release the power of the Holy Spirit to produce the transformation you desire and that He longs to see!

STUDY QUESTIONS

Study to shew thyself approved unto God, a workman that needeth not to be ashamed, rightly dividing the word of truth.
— 2 Timothy 2:15

1. What does the Bible teach in First Thessalonians 5:6-8 and Titus 2:11-14 about being "sober" — *balanced, levelheaded,* and *self-controlled?* (Also consider 1 Peter 1:13; 4:7; 5:8.) How do you think the grace of God enables you to live soberly? (Consider James 4:6; Psalm 84:11; 1 Corinthians 15:10.)

2. First Timothy 3:2 says that leaders are to be "given to hospitality," which means *having a sincere love for strangers* and *an open-home mentality*. Carefully read First John 3:17 and 18 and tell how these passages reiterate what it means to be "given to hospitality." (Also consider Isaiah 58:6,7; Luke 3:11; 12:33.)

PRACTICAL APPLICATION

But be ye doers of the word, and not hearers only,
deceiving your own selves.
—James 1:22

1. Based on what you have heard in this teaching, take a few moments to pause and ask yourself these candid questions, answering them as honestly as you can.

   • *Am I vigilant and serious-minded? Or am I intoxicated with silliness?*

   • *Am I sober, balanced, and levelheaded in my thinking? Or am I extreme?*

   • *Am I of good behavior, living an orderly life? Or am I disorganized and disorderly?*

   • *Am I loving and compassionate to strangers? Or am I cold, closed, and indifferent?*

   • *How and what am I communicating through my actions and my life?*

2. If your closest friends were asked to answer these questions about you, what might they say?

3. If you are not sure how to answer these questions, pray and ask the Holy Spirit for His perspective. Then be still and listen. What is He showing you about these areas of your life?

TOPIC

Not Addicted, No Striker

SCRIPTURES

1. **1 Timothy 3:1-3** — This is a true saying, If a man desire the office of a bishop, he desireth a good work. A bishop then must be blameless, the husband of one wife, vigilant, sober, of good behaviour, given to hospitality, apt to teach; not given to wine, no striker, not greedy of filthy lucre; but patient, not a brawler, not covetous

GREEK WORDS

1. "true" — πιστὸς (*pistos*): faithful; reliable; dependable; trustworthy

2. "a man" — τις (*tis*): anyone; either male nor female; it is not specific to male or female

3. "desire" — ὀρέγω (*orego*): to stretch forward; to reach toward; the longing, craving, urge, burning desire, or yearning ambition to achieve something or to become something; it portrays a person so fixed on the object of his desire that his entire being is stretched forward to take hold of that goal or object

4. "office of a bishop" — ἐπίσκοπος (*episkopos*): one who watches, looks, observes, or surveys; one who has oversight or who administrates or manages; a supervisory position; a visible leader

5. "good" — καλός (*kalos*): beautiful, excellent, good, noble, worthy, honorable, or virtuous; highly esteemed

6. "work" — ἔργον (*ergon*): works, deeds, or activity, conveying the idea of work that is produced by consistent and tireless effort

7. "bishop" — ἐπίσκοπος (*episkopos*): one who watches, looks, observes, or surveys; one who has oversight or who administrates or manages; a supervisory position; a visible leader

8. "must be" — δεῖ (*dei*): an obligation or necessity; absolutely must be

9. "blameless" — ἀνεπίληπτος (*anepilemptos*): regardless of how reproachful or shameful a person's actions once were, this word denotes one whose reputation has been restored; former blame has

been removed and now this individual is blameless; in spite of a lurid past, there is now nothing to disqualify this person because blame is removed, and he has become blame-free; pictures one who has no obvious flaws that would be a stumbling block to people and hinder them from following him; one with no blatant outward flaws

10. "the husband of one wife" — μιᾶς γυναικὸς ἄνδρα (*mias gunaikos andra*): literally a one-woman man; a one-woman sort of man; a man who has the character of fidelity to one woman if he is married

11. "vigilant" — νηφαλέος (*nephalios*): sober, not like a silly drunk; not intoxicated with silliness; serious-minded

12. "sober" — σωφρονέω (*sophroneo*): to be of sound mind; reasonable; balanced; levelheaded in the way one thinks

13. "good behavior" — κόσμιος (*kosmios*): from κόσμος (*kosmos*); depicts something that is ordered; it is where we get the words "cosmos" and "cosmetics"; when it becomes κόσμιος (*kosmios*), it pictures one whose life is in order; applies to every sphere of one's existence — relationships, finances, property, etc.

14. "given to hospitality" — φιλόξενος (*philoxenos*): love for a foreigner or stranger; having an open-home mentality

15. "apt to teach" — διδακτικός (*didaktikos*): pictures one who is skillful in teaching; a communicator

16. "given to wine" — πάροινος (*paroinos*): from παρά (*para*) and οἶνος (*oinos*); the word παρά (*para*) means "alongside"; the word οἶνος (*oinos*) means "wine"; compounded, one who is alongside wine; one who is alongside a bottle of wine; one who is addicted; pictures dependency upon alcohol; a chemical addiction

17. "striker" — πλήκτης (*plektes*): one who strikes; one whose temperament is explosive; an unpredictable personality

SYNOPSIS

Have you ever wondered about the origin of the word "orchestra"? It may surprise you to learn that it is directly connected with the ancient Bouleuterion we have talked about in our previous lessons. In most major cities, the Bouleuterion also functioned as an *Odeon*, which was an amphitheater-like concert hall. Situated at the very bottom of these arenas was the *orchestra* — an area where the speakers would stand and speak, and the actors would act. The orchestra was a little lower than the rest of the facility, which is why in today's modern musical halls, it is called the *orchestra pit.*

The original *Odeon* in Ephesus was constructed around 150 AD and could seat approximately 1,500 spectators. It also served as the city's *Bouleuterion*, where the members of the city council gathered to discuss governmental issues. These councilors were the elected officials of the city who were admired and trusted because of their moral character and integrity.

Similarly, those who serve in any position of leadership in the church are required to have the same high standards. In First Timothy 3, the apostle Paul wrote to Timothy and gave him — *and us* — a list of essential, practical qualifications a person needs have in order to be a leader. Let's briefly review First Timothy 3:1 and 2 and then examine some of the new criteria Paul presents in verse 3.

The emphasis of this lesson:

A leader in the church should not be given to wine or be a striker. This means he does not depend on alcohol or have a chemical addiction, and his demeanor is stable and steady — not unpredictable or explosive.

A Summary of Our Anchor Verse
First Timothy 3:1

In First Timothy 3:1 Paul stated, "This is a true saying, If a man desire the office of a bishop, he desireth a good work." We have noted the meaning of four important words or phrases in this verse:

The word **"true"** is the Greek word *pistos*, which means *faithful; reliable; dependable; trustworthy.*

The phrase **"a man"** in Greek is the word *tis*, and it describes *anyone, either male or female.* It is *gender neutral.* This paves the way for any man or any woman to serve as a leader in God's house.

The word **"desire"** is the Greek word *orego*, which means *to stretch forward* or *to reach toward.* It depicts *a longing, a craving, an urge, a burning desire, or a yearning ambition to achieve something or to become something.* It pictures *a person so fixed on the object of his desire that his entire being is stretched forward to take hold of that goal* *or object*. Desire is the foundational qualification to be a leader. A person without desire will never make it as a leader. Yet a person with desire can overcome anything.

The phrase **"office of a bishop"** is a poor translation of the original Greek. For starters, the word "office" does not appear in the text, and the word "bishop" would better be translated as *overseer*. It is the Greek word *episkopos*, a compound of the words *epi* and *skopos*. The word *epi* means *over*, and the word *skopos* means *to look*. When these words come together to form the word *episkopos*, it denotes *one who has oversight over people or over projects*. Basically, *episkopos* describes *a visible leader*.

Seven Characteristics of a Church Leader Listed in First Timothy 3:2

The apostle Paul began building the list of leader qualifications in First Timothy 3:2 declaring, "A bishop then must be blameless, the husband of one wife, vigilant, sober, of good behaviour, given to hospitality, apt to teach." Here for a second time we see the word "bishop," which is the Greek word *episkopos*, and it describes *one who watches, looks, observes, or surveys; one who has oversight or who administrates or manages; a visible leader*. Thus, a "bishop" by definition includes the pastor, as well as the worship leader, a deacon, a parking lot attendant, the church janitor, and other positions of responsibility and oversight.

Here, the Bible describes what a visible leader "must be." The phrase "must be" is the Greek word *dei*, and it describes *an obligation or necessity; something that absolutely must be*. Verse 2 then presents seven specific characteristics a leader *emphatically* must possess:

1. **"Blameless"** is the Greek word *anepilemptos*, and it denotes that regardless of how reproachful or shameful a person's actions once were, his reputation has been restored; former blame has been removed and now this individual is blameless. In spite of a lurid past, there is now nothing to disqualify this person because blame has been removed, and he has become blame-free. The word *anepilemptos* pictures *one who has no obvious flaws that would be a stumbling block to people and hinder them from following him; one with no blatant outward flaws*. A "blameless" person is one with a good reputation.

2. **"The husband of one wife"** in Greek is *mias gunaikos andra*, and it literally means *a one-woman man*; *a one-woman sort of man*; or *a man who has the character of fidelity to one woman if he is married*. For a detailed look at this word, please refer back to Lesson 5.

3. **"Vigilant"** is the Greek word *nephalios*, which means *sober, not like a silly drunk*. It is *the picture of one who is serious-minded, not intoxicated with silliness*. A person who is perceived as a silly jokester will never be taken seriously, and if he is intoxicated with silliness, he will only be able to impart silliness to others.

4. **"Sober"** in Greek is the word *sophroneo*, and it means *to be of sound mind; to be reasonable; to be balanced*. It is the picture of *one who is levelheaded in the way he or she thinks*. A leader who is "sober" will help instill *balance* and *levelheaded thinking* into those under his or her care.

5. **"Good behavior"** is the Greek word *kosmios*, from the word *kosmos*, which depicts *something that is ordered*. It is where we get the words "cosmos" and "cosmetics." When *kosmos* becomes *kosmios*, it pictures *one whose life is in order*, and it applies to every sphere of one's existence — relationships, finances, property, etc. Paul used this word to let us know that when we choose a leader, we need to look for a person who has order — not disorder — in his relationships, finances, and personal life. If his private life is chaotic, he will impart chaos into those he leads.

6. **"Given to hospitality"** is a compound of the word *philos*, which means *love*, and the word *xenos*, which describes *a stranger*. When these two words are joined together to form the word *philoxenos*, it describes *love for a foreigner or stranger* or *having an open-home mentality*. A person who offers the use of his home and resources is open and wants to serve God and His people without limitations. If a person's home is off limits, it usually indicates that he is going to have limitations in what he will do for God in the church.

7. **"Apt to teach"** is the Greek word *didaktikos*, and it pictures *one who is skillful in teaching*. This does not mean a leader has to be a verse-by-verse teacher of Scripture or a Bible scholar. It simply means he is a good communicator. Leadership is all about communication.

   When a leader shows up on time, he is communicating to everyone in his group that punctuality is important. On the contrary, when a leader is consistently late, he's teaching that promptness and other people's time are not valuable. Likewise, when a leader lifts his hands in worship or gives in the offering or serves on a community outreach, he is still communicating; people are watching and taking mental notes. This is what a person in leadership must understand — he's in a school room all the time, and the people under his supervision are like students who are always watching, listening, and learning.

'Not Given to Wine'

When we come to First Timothy 3:3, Paul added that a leader should be "Not given to wine, no striker, not greedy of filthy lucre; but patient, not a brawler, not covetous." The phrase "given to wine" is a translation of the Greek word *paroinos*. It is a compound of the word *para*, meaning *alongside*, and the word *oinos*, which is the word for *wine*. When the two words are compounded, it means *one who is alongside wine; one who is alongside a bottle of wine;* or *one who is addicted.* It pictures *dependency upon alcohol* or *a chemical addiction.*

Therefore, in this verse, Paul is clearly stating that a visible Christian leader cannot be a person who is *living alongside a bottle of wine.* That is, *he or she cannot be dependent upon alcohol or have a chemical addiction.* The reason this is so critical is, a leader cannot minister freedom to others when he himself is bound. We can only give to others what we ourselves possess.

Given the addictive nature of alcohol, and the fact that we live in a world where addictions are at an all-time high and continue to increase, why not just *abstain* from it altogether? Remember, God's Word says, "…Not all things are constructive [to character] and edifying [to spiritual life]" (1 Corinthians 10:23 *AMPC*). Hence, abstinence from alcohol is an option.

'No Striker'

After addressing the issue of drinking, Paul included that a leader must not be a "striker." This is the Greek word *plektes*, and it literally means *one who strikes with the fist or slaps with the hand.* It describes *one whose temperament is explosive; an unpredictable personality.* Although this may seem odd or out of place to include in a list of leadership qualifications, it was actually very appropriate in light of the First Century world.

When Paul wrote this letter to Timothy, there were a large number of individuals who had come to Christ out of the slave community, and slaves were accustomed to being beaten by their masters. If the master didn't like or appreciate what a slave said or did, he would often slap the slave on the side of the head. It was quite common for slaves to be struck or slapped.

As these slaves turned to Christ, many of them became leaders in the church. Sadly, the only kind of correction they knew was the harsh treatment they had received from their masters. Consequently, when these former slaves-turned-leaders experienced conflicts with other believers, they resorted to slapping and striking them. This was actually a very challenging problem in the Early Church; visible Christian leaders were slapping people who were being rude or offensive to get them back in order. Hence, when Paul said a leader can't be a "striker," that is what he was referring to.

At the same time, not being a striker (*plektes*) also means a Christian leader *cannot be explosive, abusive*, or *have an unpredictable personality*. If a leader is explosive, people will never know what he's going to be like when they see him. One moment he's glad; the next moment he's sad. At first he is joyous, but minutes later, he is raging mad. An unpredictable, explosive personality creates a very unstable environment. In fact, people who are supposed to submit to and follow a leader often struggle to do so if that leader is unstable and volatile.

As a leader, you must remember that the people under you really want to do what is right. It's a big step for them to come to church, and it's an even bigger step for them to serve at church. Usually they are giving their very best. But if they are worried about you being explosive or unpredictable — one day up and the next day down — it will make it harder for them to step forward and serve.

It's hard to be a leader when people are afraid of you. If you are struggling in this area, ask God to help you provide an emotionally stable environment for those you lead.

STUDY QUESTIONS

Study to shew thyself approved unto God, a workman that needeth not to be ashamed, rightly dividing the word of truth.
— 2 Timothy 2:15

1. Prior to this lesson, what has been your understanding regarding what the Bible says about being a Christian and drinking alcohol?

2. After hearing the meaning of the phrase "not given to wine" (*paroinos*), do you see this issue differently?

3. What wisdom can you personally glean from these passages of scripture concerning the consumption of alcohol?

   • **Proverbs 20:1; 21:17**

   • **Proverbs 23:29-35**

   • **Ephesians 5:18; Luke 1:15; Acts 10:38**

PRACTICAL APPLICATION

> But be ye doers of the word, and not hearers only,
> deceiving your own selves.
> —James 1:22

1. One of the qualifications of a Christian leader is to not be a "striker," which means a leader *cannot be explosive, abusive,* or *have an unpredictable personality.* In all honesty, how would you describe *your* personality? Would you say it's *steady* and *stable* or *unpredictable* and *explosive*? How do you think your family members, friends, and coworkers might describe it?

2. Through Paul, the Holy Spirit gives us an important standard by which we are to determine whether or not to participate in certain activities. It is found in First Corinthians 6:12 and then reiterated in 10:23. What is the essential message being communicated in these verses?

3. Are there any areas in your life that are controlling or "mastering" you in an unhealthy way? If so, where? What adjustments can you make to walk in freedom and come up higher in your relationship with Jesus?

TOPIC

Patient, Not a Brawler, Not Covetous

SCRIPTURES

1. **1 Timothy 3:1-7** — This is a true saying, If a man desire the office of a bishop, he desireth a good work. A bishop then must be blameless, the husband of one wife, vigilant, sober, of good behaviour, given to hospitality, apt to teach; not given to wine, no striker, not greedy of filthy lucre; but patient, not a brawler, not covetous; one that ruleth well his own house, having his children in subjection with all gravity; (For if a man know not how to rule his own house, how shall he take care of the church of God?) Not a novice, lest being lifted up with pride he fall into the condemnation of the devil. Moreover he must have a good report of them which are without; lest he fall into reproach and the snare of the devil.

GREEK WORDS

1. "true" — **πιστὸς** (*pistos*): faithful; reliable; dependable; trustworthy

2. "a man" — **τις** (*tis*): anyone; either male nor female; it is not specific to male or female

3. "desire" — **ὀρέγω** (*orego*): to stretch forward; to reach toward; the longing, craving, urge, burning desire, or yearning ambition to achieve something or to become something; it portrays a person so fixed on the object of his desire that his entire being is stretched forward to take hold of that goal or object

4. "office of a bishop" — **ἐπίσκοπος** (*episkopos*): one who watches, looks, observes, or surveys; one who has oversight or who administrates or manages; a supervisory position; pictures a ruler entrusted with the care of a city or country; depicts a political leader who was to provide oversight and management of a region and of all the citizens who lived in that region; depicts construction supervisors who provided oversight of construction sites, ensuring that funds were spent properly, that expenditures didn't exceed the budget, that people did their jobs correctly, and that construction of a building was done in com-

pliance with the desires of the architect; pictures one whose task is to give oversight and who is ultimately responsible for an entire project from beginning to end

5. "good" — καλός (*kalos*): beautiful, excellent, good, noble, worthy, honorable, or virtuous; highly esteemed

6. "work" — ἔργον (*ergon*): works, deeds, or activity, conveying the idea of work that is produced by consistent and tireless effort

7. "bishop" — ἐπίσκοπος (*episkopos*): one who watches, looks, observes, or surveys; one who has oversight or who administrates or manages; pictures a supervisory position; a visible leader

8. "must be" — δεῖ (*dei*): an obligation or necessity; absolutely must be

9. "blameless" — ἀνεπίληπτος (*anepilemptos*): regardless of how reproachful or shameful a person's actions once were, this word denotes one whose reputation has been restored; former blame has been removed and now this individual is blameless; in spite of a lurid past, there is now nothing to disqualify this person because blame is removed, and he has become blame-free; pictures one who has no obvious flaws that would be a stumbling block to people and hinder them from following him; one with no blatant outward flaws

10. "the husband of one wife" — μιᾶς γυναικὸς ἄνδρα (*mias gunaikos andra*): literally a one-woman man; a one-woman sort of man; a man who has the character of fidelity to one woman if he is married

11. "vigilant" — νηφαλέος (*nephalios*): sober, not like a silly drunk; not intoxicated with silliness; serious-minded

12. "sober" — σωφρονέω (*sophroneo*): to be of sound mind; reasonable; balanced; levelheaded in the way one thinks

13. "good behavior" — κόσμιος (*kosmios*): from κόσμος (*kosmos*); depicts something that is ordered; it is where we get the words "cosmos" and "cosmetics"; when it becomes κόσμιος (*kosmios*), it pictures one whose life is in order; applies to every sphere of one's existence — relationships, finances, property, etc.

14. "given to hospitality" — φιλόξενος (*philoxenos*): love for a foreigner or stranger; having an open-home mentality

15. "apt to teach" — διδακτικός (*didaktikos*): pictures one who is skillful in teaching; a communicator

16. "given to wine" — πάροινος (*paroinos*): from παρά (*para*) and οἶνος (*oinos*); the word παρά (*para*) means "alongside"; the word οἶνος

(*oinos*) means "wine"; compounded, one who is alongside wine; one who is alongside a bottle of wine; one who is addicted; pictures dependency upon alcohol; a chemical addiction

17. "striker" — **πλήκτης** (*plektes*): one who strikes; one whose temperament is explosive; an unpredictable personality

18. "patient" — **ἐπιεικής** (*epieikes*): gentle; mild; restrained

19. "not a brawler" — **ἄμαχος** (*amachos*): an **ᾰ** (*a*) attached to **μάχομαι** (*machomai*); the word **μάχομαι** (*machomai*) depicts a battle, fight, or war, usually a war of words; pictures one who wrangles with words; conversations filled with strife; but **ἄμαχος** depicts one who refuses to fight with words or wrangle with words, or; pictures one who turns down opportunities to get caught up in a war of words

20. "not coveteous" — **ἀφιλάργυρος** (*aphilarguros*): an **ᾰ** (*a*) with attached to **φιλάργυρος** (*philarguros*); the word **φιλάργυρος** (*philarguros*) pictures an inordinate love for money or a fixation on material possessions; when it becomes **ἀφιλάργυρος** (*aphilarguros*), it pictures one who is free from the love of money; one who does not have a preoccupation with money or a fixation on material possessions

SYNOPSIS

If you were able to journey back in time 2,000 years and peer into the Bouleuterion in the upper district of Ephesus, you would see dignified men dressed in exquisite Roman togas taking their seats in the city council to discuss, debate, and decide on public policies. It was an honor and privilege to be a part of the *boule*, or parliament, of the city. And yet, being a leader in the house of God was — *and is* — an even greater privilege!

In early New Testament times, the church of Ephesus experienced a real leadership crisis. Timothy, who was pastoring the church at that time, had just removed a number of rebellious leaders who had wandered away from the truth and had begun teaching false doctrine. He needed to fill their positions of authority with qualified leaders. After reaching out to the apostle Paul for guidance, Paul provided him a practical list of requirements. Thus far, we have looked at nine qualifications. Let's briefly review these and look at three additional attributes that appear in the latter part of First Timothy 3:3.

The emphasis of this lesson:

According to Scripture, a leader in the church is to be patient, not a brawler, and not covetous. This means exercising restraint of one's emotions, choosing not to get roped into a war of words with others, and keeping his life free from the love of money and material possessions.

A Brief Review of Our Anchor Verse
First Timothy 3:1

In response to Timothy's request for wisdom in choosing leaders, the apostle Paul wrote and said, "This is a true saying, If a man desire the office of a bishop, he desireth a good work." Here is a summary of the meanings of six key words and phrases in this verse:

"True" is the Greek word *Pistos*, which means *faithful; reliable; dependable; trustworthy*. What Paul was about to say regarding leaders could be fully trusted.

"A man" in Greek is the word *tis*, and it describes *anyone, either male or female*. It is *not gender specific*. A better translation of this part of the verse would be, *"If anyone desires the office of a bishop."*

"Desire" is the Greek word *orego*, which means *to stretch forward* or *to reach toward*. It describes *a longing, a craving, a burning desire, or a yearning ambition to achieve something or to become something*. It pictures *a person so fixed on the object of his desire that his entire being is stretched forward to take hold of it*. A person with "desire" cannot be held back from obtaining or achieving their goal.

"Office of a bishop" is the phrase that appears in the *King James Version*, but it is not an accurate translation. In the original Greek, the word "office" doesn't appear. It simply says "bishop," which in Greek is the word *episkopos*. It is a compound of the words *epi* and *skopos*. The word *epi* means *over*, and the word *skopos* means *to look*. When they are compounded to form the word *episkopos*, it depicts *one who has oversight over people or over projects; a visible leader*.

"Good" is the Greek word *kalos*, and it describes *something beautiful, excellent, good, honorable, noble, worthy, or highly esteemed*. Desiring to be a leader is "good."

"Work" in Greek is the word *ergon*. It indicates *works, deeds, or activity, conveying the idea of work that is produced by consistent and tireless effort.*

Seven Practical Prerequisites of a Leader in the Church
Seen in First Timothy 3:2

Building on the six qualifications in verse 1, Paul added, "A bishop then must be blameless, the husband of one wife, vigilant, sober, of good behaviour, given to hospitality, apt to teach" (1 Timothy 3:2). Again, the word "bishop" — the Greek word *episkopos* — appears. It describes *one who watches, looks, observes, or surveys; one who has oversight or who administrates or manages; a visible leader.*

Paul then listed seven qualities in verse 2 of what a leader "must be." The phrase "must be" is the Greek word *dei*, meaning *an obligation or necessity; something that emphatically must be.* What characteristics are absolutely mandatory for a leader to possess? They are listed as follows:

- **"Blameless"** — This is the Greek word *anepilemptos*, and it denotes that *regardless of how reproachful or shameful a person's actions once were, his reputation has been restored*; his former blame has been removed and now he is blameless. In spite of a lurid past, there is now nothing to disqualify this person because blame has been removed, and he has become blame-free. The word *anepilemptos* pictures *one who has no obvious outward flaws that would be a stumbling block to people and hinder them from following him.* A "blameless" person is one with a good reputation.

- **"The husband of one wife"** — In Greek, this literally means *a one-woman man; a one-woman sort of man*; or *a man who has the character of fidelity to one woman if he is married.* For a comprehensive examination of this word, please refer back to Lesson 5.

- **"Vigilant"** — This is the Greek word *nephalios*, which describes *one who is sober, not like a silly drunk.* It depicts *one who is serious-minded* or *not intoxicated with silliness.* A leader who is viewed as a silly jokester will never be taken seriously. Moreover, if he is filled with silliness, he will only have silliness to give to others.

- **"Sober"** — In Greek, this is the word *sophroneo*, meaning *to be of sound mind; to be reasonable; to be balanced.* It denotes *one who is not extreme but levelheaded in the way he or she thinks.* A "sober" leader will inject balance and levelheaded thinking into those he or she leads.

- **"Good behavior"** — This phrase is a translation of the Greek word *kosmios*, which is from the word *kosmos.* It pictures *something that is ordered* or *orderly*, and it is from where we get the words "cosmos" and "cosmetics." When *kosmos* becomes *kosmios*, it denotes *one whose life is in order* in every sphere of his existence. Paul uses this word to inform us that when we choose a leader, we must look for a person who has *order* in his relationships, finances, and personal life. If a person's private life is chaotic, he is going to impart chaos to the people under his care.

- **"Given to hospitality"** — In Greek, these words are a compound of the word *philos*, which means *love*, and the word *xenos*, which is the word for *a stranger.* When the new word — *philoxenos* — is formed, it describes *love for a foreigner or stranger; having an open-home mentality.*

- **"Apt to teach"** — This phrase is the Greek word *didaktikos*, and it pictures *one who is skillful in teaching; an effective communicator.* Leaders must realize that their lives are their pulpit, and they are constantly communicating through their actions. Leadership is all about communication.

A Leader Must Not Be 'Given to Wine' or 'a Striker'

In our last lesson, we saw that a leader is also "Not given to wine, no striker…" (1 Timothy 3:3). The words "given to wine" is the Greek word *paroinos*, which is a compound of the word *para*, meaning "alongside," and the word *oinos*, meaning "wine." When the words are compounded to become *paroinos*, it depicts *one who is alongside wine; one who is alongside a bottle of wine;* or *one who is addicted.* It indicates *dependency upon alcohol* or *a chemical addiction.*

Today, people have easy access to not only alcohol, but also drugs, medications, and many other addictive substances. Restaurants, convenience stores, and supermarkets are all well stocked with a plethora of prepackaged "spirits" available for immediate consumption. Likewise, a number of states and territories have legalized marijuana, giving way to its farming and widespread distribution. In this verse, the Holy Spirit speaks through

Paul and declares that a visible Christian leader cannot be dependent upon alcohol or have a chemical addiction. The reason is clear: a leader cannot minister freedom to others when he himself is bound. We can only give to others what we ourselves possess.

Moreover, Paul added that a leader must not be a "striker," which is the Greek word *plektes*, and it literally means *one who strikes with the fist or slaps with the hand*. It also describes *one whose personality is explosive and unpredictable*. Although this may seem strange to list as a requirement for Christian leaders, Paul had good reason for including it.

In the First Century, there were many people who came to Christ out of the slave community, and as slaves they were accustomed to being beaten by their masters. If a master didn't like or appreciate what a slave said or did, he would slap or strike them in any way he pleased. As these slaves turned to Christ, many of them became leaders in the church. Sadly, the only style of leadership they knew was the kind they'd observed from their masters. Consequently, when these former slaves became leaders, they began slapping and striking church members that were out of line. Hence, when Paul said a leader can't be a "striker," that is what he was referring to.

Additionally, not being a "striker" (*plektes*) meant a Christian leader cannot be *explosive*, *abusive*, or *have an unpredictable personality*. The truth is, it is very difficult to follow and serve under a leader who is explosive and unpredictable. You can't focus on ministering to others when you are worried and distracted by the possibility of what your leader might do. An unpredictable, explosive personality creates a very unstable environment.

People who are supposed to submit to and follow their leaders won't want to if the leaders are volatile. It's hard to be an effective leader when people are afraid of you.

A Leader Is To Be 'Patient, Not a Brawler, and Not Covetous'

What other qualifications did Paul establish for leaders? He said they must be "...patient, not a brawler, not covetous" (1 Timothy 3:3). The word "patient" in Greek is *epieikes*, and it means *gentle*; *mild*; *restrained*. Hence, one who is "patient" is one who is able to restrain his emotions, which includes the ability to control one's mouth. This tells us that leaders cannot just say anything that pops into their head. They must exercise restraint.

James 3:2 (*CEV*) says, "...If you can control your tongue, you are mature and able to control your whole body."

Furthermore, a leader is not to be a "brawler." The phrase "not a brawler" is a translation of the Greek word *amachos*, which is the word *machomai* with an *a* attached to the front of it. The word *machomai* depicts *a battle, fight, or war — usually a war of words*. It pictures *one who wrangles with words* or *conversations filled with strife*. In this instance, the "a" attached to the front of the word cancels its meaning. Thus the word *amachos* depicts *one who refuses to fight with words or wrangle with words* or *one who turns down opportunities to get caught up in a war of words*.

Like it or not, when you're in leadership, there will be times when people want to fight you. As a leader, you have to be "patient" (*epieikes*) and not a "brawler" (*amachos*). You must exercise restraint and make a decision that regardless of what anyone else says, you are not going to get dragged into a war of words. If you take the bait and engage in a verbal battle, you will sink to a low level — don't go there. Take the high road of restraint and be patient.

The last leadership qualification Paul mentions in First Timothy 3:3 is to not be "coveteous," which in Greek is the word *aphilarguros*. The word *philarguros* pictures *an inordinate love for money* or *a fixation on material possessions*. When an "a" is attached to *philarguros* and it becomes *aphilarguros*, it pictures *one who is free from the love of money; one who does not have a preoccupation with money or a fixation on material possessions*.

So in the first three verses of First Timothy 3, there are *13 qualifications* that are required of anyone who desires to serve as a leader in God's house. Do you have these operating in your life? If you don't, you can cooperate with the Holy Spirit and develop them! God is calling you to rise up and become a visible leader in every sphere of influence in which you walk.

STUDY QUESTIONS

Study to shew thyself approved unto God, a workman that needeth not to be ashamed, rightly dividing the word of truth.
— 2 Timothy 2:15

1. Take a few moments to reread First Timothy 3:1-3 and identify the *13 qualifications* for being a visible leader in the church. Which of

these can you see operating in your life? Which one(s) would you say are most lacking and need to be developed?

2. One who is "patient" is one who is able to *restrain* his emotions, which includes the ability to control one's mouth. According to these scriptures, what benefits can you expect from learning to yield your tongue to the control of God's Spirit?

- **Psalm 34:12-14; 1 Peter 3:10,11**

- **Proverbs 10:19; 11:12; 17:27; 18:6,7**

- **Proverbs 11:13; 17:9; 1 Peter 4:8**

- **Proverbs 13:2,3; 21:23**

3. Being *covetous* means having *an inordinate love for money* or *a fixation on material possessions*. Take a moment to meditate on the liberating truth found in First Timothy 6:6-11. What does this passage reveal as the key to avoiding the trap of covetousness? (Also consider Jesus' words in Matthew 6:33 and the promise of Hebrews 13:5.) Pray and ask the Lord to develop this protective virtue in you.

PRACTICAL APPLICATION

**But be ye doers of the word, and not hearers only,
deceiving your own selves.**
— James 1:22

1. Have you ever had to follow and serve a leader who was *explosive* and *unpredictable*? How about one who *lacked patience* or was a "brawler"? If so, describe what it was like.

2. How did God help you navigate and make it through that difficult situation? What words of encouragement could you offer a close friend who is presently experiencing such a challenge?

TOPIC

Rules Well His Own Home, Respectable Children

SCRIPTURES

1. **1 Timothy 3:1-7** — This is a true saying, If a man desire the office of a bishop, he desireth a good work. A bishop then must be blameless, the husband of one wife, vigilant, sober, of good behaviour, given to hospitality, apt to teach; not given to wine, no striker, not greedy of filthy lucre; but patient, not a brawler, not covetous; one that ruleth well his own house, having his children in subjection with all gravity; (For if a man know not how to rule his own house, how shall he take care of the church of God?) Not a novice, lest being lifted up with pride he fall into the condemnation of the devil. Moreover he must have a good report of them which are without; lest he fall into reproach and the snare of the devil.

GREEK WORDS

1. "true" — πιστὸς (*pistos*): faithful; reliable; dependable; trustworthy
2. "a man" — τις (*tis*): anyone; either male nor female; it is not specific to male or female
3. "desire" — ὀρέγω (*orego*): to stretch forward; to reach toward; the longing, craving, urge, burning desire, or yearning ambition to achieve something or to become something; it portrays a person so fixed on the object of his desire that his entire being is stretched forward to take hold of that goal or object
4. "office of a bishop" — ἐπίσκοπος (*episkopos*): one who watches, looks, observes, or surveys; one who has oversight or who administrates or manages; a supervisory position; pictures a ruler entrusted with the care of a city or country; depicts a political leader who was to provide oversight and management of a region and of all the citizens who lived in that region; depicts construction supervisors who provided oversight of construction sites, ensuring that funds were spent properly, that expenditures didn't exceed the budget, that people did their

jobs correctly, and that construction of a building was done in compliance with the desires of the architect; pictures one whose task is to give oversight and who is ultimately responsible for an entire project from beginning to end

5. "good" — καλός (*kalos*): beautiful, excellent, good, noble, worthy, honorable, or virtuous; highly esteemed

6. "work" — ἔργον (*ergon*): works, deeds, or activity, conveying the idea of work that is produced by consistent and tireless effort

7. "ruleth" — προΐστημι (*proistimi*): one who stands before others in order to lead, guide, direct, or manage a situation; a leader who responsibly gives oversight and direction; any type of leader, at home, business, government, or church; to be put up front to protect and to serve as a shield for others

8. "well" — καλῶς (*kalos*): in a way that is viewed as good; well-perceived; appealing or attractive to others

9. "house" — οἶκος (*oikos*): a physical house; a household, including the residents of the house, the management of the house, and the physical state of the house; the bills connected everything that happens in a house; everything about a person's residence and home life

10. "children" — τέκνον (*teknon*): children who are still under parental guidance at home; pictures a non-adult child who remains at home and is under the authority of parents; children who are still under parental guidance

11. "subjection" — ὑποταγή (*hupotage*): to set things in order; to be subject to a defined order; obedience to authority; a military term that was used to describe soldiers who were under the command or authority of a superior officer; implies knowing one's place, function, and assignment in an army or any type of organization or relationship; one who is submitted to some type of authority and is expected to act according to that order of authority

12. "gravity" — σεμνότης (*semnotes*): one who carries himself with dignity and treats other people with courtesy and respect; to be cultured and polite in one's treatment of others; how an individual speaks, carries himself, and treats others reveals whether or not he or she has this trait

13. "a man" — τις (*tis*): anyone; either male nor female; not specific to male or female

14. "rule" — **προΐστημι** (*proistimi*): one who stands before others in order to lead, guide, direct, or manage a situation; a leader who responsibly gives oversight and direction; any type of leader, at home, business, government, or church; to be put up front to protect and to serve as a shield for others

15. "own house" — **ἰδίου οἴκου** (*idiou oikou*): his own private, personal life, family, and household affairs; pictures maintenance of the home, payment of bills, and to provide visible leadership to the family

SYNOPSIS

In the First Century, the ancient city of Ephesus was simply magnificent! A careful study of its ruins today reveals the immensity and splendor of its buildings. For instance, consider the enormous size of the columns that were once a part of the basilica and the remnants of the massive cornice that lined the interior of the ancient agora, the city's renowned marketplace. The exquisite detail of the mosaics, porticoes, and frescos of the luxurious establishments was truly remarkable.

Just behind the ancient basilica was the Bouleuterion. Again, this word is a derivative of the word *boules*, which means *to counsel*, and it describes the place where the prestigious councilors of Ephesus gathered regularly to deal with the city's issues and establish its public policies. To serve among this prestigious group of magistrates was a high honor. One had to possess strong character and integrity to be a leader in the city.

What was true of the city leaders is even truer concerning leadership in the Church. Contrary to what you may think, being a leader in God's house does not require a Bible school diploma or a seminary degree. However, there are some specific requirements a leader must have that were described to us by the apostle Paul in First Timothy 3. Thus far, we have covered 13 qualifications for leaders in the first three verses. To all these, Paul added, "One that ruleth well his own house, having his children in subjection with all gravity" (1 Timothy 3:4).

The emphasis of this lesson:

When considering someone to be a leader in the church, it is vital to look at the health of his home life. The condition of a person's marriage and how he is raising his children are good indicators of how he is going to manage responsibilities in God's house.

A Review of Our Anchor Verse
First Timothy 3:1

"This is a true saying, If a man desire the office of a bishop, he desireth a good work."

1 Timothy 3:1

We noted that the word "true" describes *something that is faithful, dependable, reliable, and trustworthy*. It was the equivalent of Paul saying, "Timothy, take what I'm about to tell you as a good rule of thumb. You can depend on it to be a reliable, faithful saying. If a man desires the office of a bishop, he desireth a good work." We have seen that the word "bishop" is the Greek word *episkopos*, and while it may sound religious, it is not. It's a secular word formed from the word *epi*, which means *over*, and the word *skopos*, which means *to look*. When these two words are compounded to become *episkopos*, it means *to look over* and describes *any person who has a position of management, administration, or supervision over either people or projects*.

In the secular world, examples of a "bishop" (*episkopos*) include:

- The leader of a nation, such as a president or prime minister, who has oversight of everything
- The mayor of a city or the governor of a state
- A construction-site supervisor whose job is to give oversight to an entire building project

When it comes to the church, leaders are very similar to construction-site supervisors. They work diligently to help "build" the house of God. Although they are not carrying out every detail of the work themselves, they are giving oversight to the building up of the church. Thus, the word *episkopos* — translated here as "bishop" and as "overseer" in Acts 20:28 — is a very appropriate word to describe *anyone in a visible leadership position who has oversight of people or projects*. This would include the pastor, the choir director, a Sunday school teacher, a parking lot attendant, and the church janitor.

The Bible says, "…If a man desire the office of a bishop, he desireth a good work" (1 Timothy 3:1). Again, the words "a man" is the Greek word *tis*, and it means *anyone, either male or female*; it is *not gender specific*. Therefore, any man or woman who yearns to be a visible leader in the church desires a "good work." The word "good" is the Greek word *kalos*, which means *excellent, good, or honorable*. And the word "work" in Greek is the word *ergon*, and *it conveys the idea of consistent and tireless work or activity.*

> **"A bishop then must be blameless, the husband of one wife, vigilant, sober, of good behaviour, given to hospitality, apt to teach."**
>
> **— 1 Timothy 3:2**

Paul said there are certain things a visible leader — a "bishop" — "must be." The phrase "must be" is the Greek word *dei*, and it describes *an obligation or necessity; something that absolutely must be*. First, he must be "blameless," which does not mean he's perfect. It simply means there's no defect in his life so obvious that it would hinder other people from following him. Basically, this describes a person who has a good reputation in the eyes of others. Second, it says he must be "the husband of one wife." We've seen that in Greek this literally means *a one-woman sort of guy —* an individual who is committed to his current marriage.

Next, the Bible says a leader must be "vigilant," which means *serious-minded and not intoxicated with silliness*. He also must be "sober," which in the Greek describes *one who is balanced, levelheaded in his thinking, and not extreme*. Moreover, a leader is one who exhibits "good behavior," which is the Greek word *kosmios*, and it denotes *one who has order in every area of his life*. Keep in mind, what a leader has operating in his personal life is what he is going to replicate in the lives of those he oversees. What is on the head — the leader — is what will come on the body. This is the principle of Psalm 133:2.

Paul also said that a leader should be "given to hospitality," which means he has *an open-home mentality*. If a person puts a lot of restrictions on the use of his home and resources, he will more than likely have many limitations on how far he will go in serving in the church.

The last quality Paul noted in First Timothy 3:2 is that leaders are to be "apt to teach." Basically, this means that a leader understands that his life is his pulpit, and he is teaching all the time. The people under his care are closely watching how he lives his life, and they will mirror what he is modeling before them.

"Not given to wine, no striker, not greedy of filthy lucre; but patient, not a brawler, not covetous."

1 Timothy 3:3

In verse 3, Paul began by addressing the issue of drinking. The phrase "not given to wine" is the Greek word *paroinos*, and it means *one who is along-side of a bottle; one who has a dependency upon alcohol;* or any kind of *chemical addiction.* Here, Paul was admonishing Timothy not to choose anyone for spiritual leadership who was dealing with some kind of addiction. God is not against that person; He loves them. But a person can only minister freedom to others when he himself is free. Therefore, choose people who are free so they can minister freedom to others.

Next, the Bible says a leader is not to be a "striker." This is the Greek word *plektes*, which in the First Century literally meant *to strike or slap someone.* It also carries the idea of *a person whose temperament is explosive* or *unpredictable.* People with an unpredictable personality are very difficult to follow and serve. You can't focus on ministering to others when you are worried and distracted by how your leader may or may not react. Hence, Paul instructed us to be sure to choose leaders whose temperaments are balanced.

Scripture goes on to say a leader must be "…patient, not a brawler, not covetous" (1 Timothy 3:3). The word "patient" in Greek is *epieikes,* and it means *gentle; mild;* or *restrained.* Thus, one who is "patient" is *one who is able to control his emotions,* which includes maintaining control of one's mouth. A leader is also not to be a "brawler," which is a picture of *one who refuses to fight with words* or *one who turns down opportunities to get caught up in a war of words.* Lastly, a leader is to not be "coveteous," which in Greek is the word *aphilarguros,* and it pictures *one who is free from the love of money; one who does not have a preoccupation with money or a fixation on material possessions.*

A Leader 'Ruleth Well His Own House'

In First Timothy 3:4, the apostle Paul shifted his focus toward the home and stated that a leader must be "One that ruleth well his own house…." The word "ruleth" here is the Greek word *proistimi*, and it depicts *one who stands before others in order to lead, guide, direct, or manage a situation; a leader who responsibly gives oversight and direction.* This word describes *any type of leader at home, in business, in government, or in the church.* The word *proistimi* can also mean *to be put up front to protect and to serve as a shield for others.*

By using this word, Paul was saying, "Before you put someone in charge of an area of the church, you need to first look and see how that person is leading at home. Are they a visible leader, serving as a shield of protection for their spouse and children? Are they managing their home well? Or have they abdicated their position of leadership?"

This brings us to the word "well," which is the Greek word *kalos*, and it means *in a way that is viewed as good; well-perceived.* A good leader is one who is *appealing or attractive to others* in the way he is leading his house. Interestingly, even the word "house" is important. It is the Greek word *oikos*, which describes *a household, including the residents of the house as well as the physical house itself.* This word takes into account *the management of the house, the physical state of the house, the bills connected with the house,* and *everything that happens in the house.* The word *oikos* encompasses *everything about a person's residence and home life.*

According to Scripture, leadership is formed in the home. If a person is not giving proper attention to his family, and his relationships are crumbling all around him, it is not a good sign. Likewise, if the sink is always filled with dishes, the plumbing never works, and the rooms constantly look like a warzone, then this person is probably not someone you want to be a leader in the church. Remember, this individual can only give to others what he has operating in his own life. If his leadership is producing chaos and confusion at home, that is what he will bring into the church.

A Leader's Children Should Honor and Respect Authority

In addition to ruling his house well, Paul said a leader must have "… his children in subjection with all gravity" (1 Timothy 3:4). The word "children" in this verse is the Greek word *teknon*, and it describes *children who are still under parental guidance at home.* It pictures *a non-adult child who remains at home and is under the authority of parents.* Although a parent can't be held accountable for what their adult children do, they are accountable for the behavior of their young children still under their care.

One of the most important qualities to look for in the home of a person you are considering to be a leader is the level of honor and respect the children have for authority. If the children have little to no respect for authority — if they don't honor and submit to their parents and others over them — it is an indication that the parents do not understand the importance of respect and submission to authority.

Again, a leader's children are to be "…in subjection with all gravity" (1 Timothy 3:4). The word "subjection" in Greek is *hupotage*, and it means *to set things in order; to be subject to a defined order; obedience to authority*. This is *a military term that was used to describe soldiers who were under the command or authority of a superior officer;* it implies *knowing one's place, function, and assignment in an army or any type of organization or relationship.*

A leader's children are to live in subjection to their parents with all "gravity." In Greek, the word "gravity" is *semnotes*, and it describes *one who carries himself with dignity and treats other people with courtesy and respect*. It carries the idea of *being cultured and polite in one's treatment of others*. How an individual speaks, carries himself, and treats others reveals whether or not he or she has this trait.

So, do the children of a potential leader speak to adults with respect or disrespect? Do they speak to and treat their elders as *equals* or as *superiors* in their position? Again, if the children don't have this line of behavior right, the parents probably don't have it right either.

The Way One Rules His House Will Be the Way He Leads Others in the Church

To make sure we understand the message the Holy Spirit is conveying, He prompts Paul in the very next verse to write, "For if a man know not how to rule his own house, how shall he take care of the church of God?" (1 Timothy 3:5.)

The words "a man" are again the Greek word *tis*, meaning *anyone; either male or female; not gender specific*. "Rule" is the Greek word *proistimi* — the same word used in verse First Timothy 3:4 — and it describes *one who stands before others in order to lead, guide, direct, or manage a situation; a leader who responsibly gives oversight and direction*. In this case, it specifically refers to the rule of one's "own house." In Greek, the phrase "own house" is *idiou oikou*, and it describes *one's own private, personal life, family, and household affairs*. It pictures *the maintenance of the home, payment of bills, and providing visible leadership to the family*.

To be clear, the apostle Paul is was not making a condemning statement in verse 5. He is simply saying if a person cannot lead well in the affairs of his home and the management of his family, it is foolish to think that he will be able to lead well in the church. In our final lesson, we will look at the meaning of the word "novice" and why the Bible says this type of person should *not* be placed in leadership.

STUDY QUESTIONS

Study to shew thyself approved unto God, a workman that needeth not to be ashamed, rightly dividing the word of truth.
— 2 Timothy 2:15

1. What instruction does God give to *children* in Colossians 3:20; Ephesians 6:1-3; Proverbs 1:8, and 23:22?

2. What instruction does God give you *as a parent* in His Word?

    - **Deuteronomy 6:6-9; Psalm 78:4-8**

    - **Proverbs 22:6 and Ephesians 6:4**

    - **Proverbs 13:24 and 22:15**

    - **Proverbs 19:18 and 23:13**

3. If you have younger children under your care, do they show honor and respect for authority (*see* Leviticus 19:32)? Do they honor and submit to *your* authority? What does God say in Ephesians 6:1-3 will happen if they honor and submit to you?

PRACTICAL APPLICATION

But be ye doers of the word, and not hearers only, deceiving your own selves.
— James 1:22

The Bible says that a leader "…ruleth well his own house…" (1 Timothy 3:4). This means he stands before his family and leads, guides, directs, and manages them well. He is a leader who responsibly gives oversight and direction to all aspects of his home life. How are you doing in this vital area? Are you leading your home well? Take a few moments to honestly answer these questions.

- Are you a visible leader in your home, serving as a shield of protection for your spouse and children? Or have you abdicated your frontline position?

- How are you managing your bills? Are you paying them on time, or are they delinquent?

- What about the physical upkeep of your house? Are you staying up to date on making repairs, or have things been in shambles for a while?

- How are you leading your family spiritually? Do you attend church regularly? Do you pray and have family devotionals together?

- What are you doing as a leader in your home that is attractive or appealing to others?

TOPIC

Not a Novice, Good Reputation With Unbelievers

SCRIPTURES

1. **1 Timothy 3:1-7** — This is a true saying, If a man desire the office of a bishop, he desireth a good work. A bishop then must be blameless, the husband of one wife, vigilant, sober, of good behaviour, given to hospitality, apt to teach; not given to wine, no striker, not greedy of filthy lucre; but patient, not a brawler, not covetous; one that ruleth well his own house, having his children in subjection with all gravity; (For if a man know not how to rule his own house, how shall he take care of the church of God?) Not a novice, lest being lifted up with pride he fall into the condemnation of the devil. Moreover he must have a good report of them which are without; lest he fall into reproach and the snare of the devil.

GREEK WORDS

1. "true" — **πιστὸς** (*pistos*): faithful; reliable; dependable; trustworthy

2. "a man" — **τις** (*tis*): anyone; either male nor female; it is not specific to male or female

3. "desire" — **ὀρέγω** (*orego*): to stretch forward; to reach toward; the longing, craving, urge, burning desire, or yearning ambition to achieve something or to become something; it portrays a person so fixed on the object of his desire that his entire being is stretched forward to take hold of that goal or object

4. "office of a bishop" — **ἐπίσκοπος** (*episkopos*): one who watches, looks, observes, or surveys; one who has oversight or who administrates or manages; a supervisory position; pictures a ruler entrusted with the care of a city or country; depicts a political leader who was to provide oversight and management of a region and of all the citizens who lived in that region; depicts construction supervisors who provided oversight of construction sites, ensuring that funds were spent properly, that expenditures didn't exceed the budget, that people did their jobs correctly, and that construction of a building was done in compliance with the desires of the architect; pictures one whose task is to give oversight and who is ultimately responsible for an entire project from beginning to end

5. "good" — **καλός** (*kalos*): beautiful, excellent, good, noble, worthy, honorable, or virtuous; highly esteemed

6. "work" — **ἔργον** (*ergon*): works, deeds, or activity, conveying the idea of work that is produced by consistent and tireless effort

7. "novice" — **νεόφυτος** (*neophutos*): a new plant; understood to mean a new convert or a new Christian; can refer to an old plant that is new in one's garden; a transplant; a new arrival

8. "lifted up with pride" — **τυφλόω** (*tuphloo*): blind; doesn't just depict a person who is unable to see, but a person who has been intentionally blinded by someone else; one whose eyes have been deliberately removed so that he is blinded; this individual hasn't just lost his sight — he has no eyes to see; it's where we derive the word "typhoon"

9. "fall into" — **ἐμπίπτω** (*empipto*): to fall into; to collapse into; a downward plummet into; to fall into a terrible predicament; someone who falls into some type of failure; a downfall from a presumed high and haughty position

10. "condemnation" — **κρίμα** (*krima*): verdict; sentence; judgment; condemnation

11. "devil" — **διάβολος** (*diabolos*): devil; slanderer; accusers; slanderer

12. "must" — δεῖ (*dei*): an obligation or necessity; absolutely must be

13. "have" — ἔχω (*echo*): to hold; to have; to be in possession of

14. "good report" — μαρτυρίαν καλὴν (*marturian kalen*): a good testimony; a good witness; an appealing or attractive witness

15. "of" — ἀπὸ (*apo*): coming from

16. "without" — ἔξωθεν (*exothen*): those on the outside; those outside of Christ; refers to non-church members or non-Christians

SYNOPSIS

During the First Century, the population of the city of Ephesus was huge. In fact, it was the fourth largest city in the entire Roman Empire, brimming with nearly 200,000 residents. The upper district of Ephesus was populated with rich, influential people whose homes extended all the way up the mountainsides. This was the same area where the magnificent Bouleuterion was located. As we've seen, the Bouleuterion was the gathering place where the distinguished *boules*, or city counselors, met to make important decisions that governed the citizens.

Ephesus was also home to the world's largest church. It was founded through the tireless efforts of the apostle Paul along with the help of his Hebrew friends Aquila and Priscilla. Years later, Paul appointed Timothy to serve as the pastor at Ephesus. It was during his tenure that a number of leaders got off track and began teaching false doctrine. When they refused to repent and realign themselves with the truth of Scripture, Timothy removed them and replaced them with new, qualified leaders. Paul assisted in the selection process by providing a practical list of requirements for anyone who wanted to serve as a leader in the church.

Let's review the qualifications for leaders in the first five verses of First Timothy 3 once more. Then we will turn our attention to Paul's additional instructions in verse 6 and 7 and learn what a "novice" is and why we should never place a novice in a position of authority.

The emphasis of this lesson:

Paul said we are not to make a novice a leader in God's house. Although a novice does refer to a new believer, it can also denote a new arrival in a church. Appointing a novice to a position of leadership can release a spiritual storm within a church.

A Final Review of *First Timothy 3:1-5*

"This is a true saying, If a man desire the office of a bishop, he desireth a good work."

1 Timothy 3:1

We've seen that the word "true" is the Greek word *pistos*, and it describes *something faithful, reliable, dependable, and trustworthy*. Paul's choice to use the word *pistos* was the equivalent of saying, "Here is a set of reliable guidelines on how to choose leaders; you can count on them to always be true."

Then he said, "…If a man desire the office of a bishop, he desireth a good work." We have noted that the words "a man" is the Greek word *tis*, and it describes *anyone, either male or female*. And the word "desire" is the Greek word *orego*, which means *to stretch forward* or *to reach toward*, and it depicts *one with a burning desire or yearning ambition to achieve or become something*. Thus, if any man or woman yearns and longs for the office of a "bishop," he or she desireth a good work.

The word "bishop" is the Greek word *episkopos*, which is a compound of the word *epi*, meaning *over*, and the word *skopos*, meaning *to look* or *to see*. *Skopos* is from where we get the word "scope" — as in *microscope* and *telescope*. When you compound *epi* and *skopos* to form the word *episkopos*, it describes *one who watches, looks over, observes, or surveys a situation*. It is *any person who has an administrative position, a managerial position or a position where he supervises people or projects*. It pictures *a ruler entrusted with the care of a city or country, such as a mayor or a president*.

The word *episkopos* was specifically used to describe those who were construction-site supervisors. Although these administrators didn't physically build the building, they had oversight over every aspect of the project from start to finish. The buck stopped with them. In the New Testament, the word *episkopos* is translated as the word "overseers" in Acts 20:28 and as the word "bishop" here in First Timothy 3:1. This was not originally a religious term but a secular term that described a visible leader.

Thus Paul told Timothy, "Anyone — male or female — who desires to serve as a visible leader in the church, desires a good work." The word "good" is the Greek word *kalos*, which describes *something beautiful, excellent, or honorable*; and the word "work" in Greek is *ergon*, which denotes *consistent hard work*.

"A bishop then must be blameless, the husband of one wife, vigilant, sober, of good behaviour, given to hospitality, apt to teach; not given to wine, no striker, not greedy of filthy lucre; but patient, not a brawler, not covetous."

1 Timothy 3:2,3

We examined the meaning of the words "blameless" in Lesson 4; "the husband of one wife" in Lesson 5; and "vigilant, sober, of good behavior, given to hospitality, apt to teach" in Lesson 6. Please refer back to these lessons to refresh your memory and reinforce your understanding of these words and phrases.

The phrase "not given to wine" is a translation of the Greek word *paroinos*, which means *one who is alongside wine; one who is alongside a bottle of wine; or one who is addicted*. It pictures *dependency upon alcohol* or *a chemical addiction*. And the words "no striker" is from the Greek word *plektes*, indicating *one whose temperament is not explosive or unpredictable; one whose personality is stable*. For a more detailed look at these phrases, please refer back to Lesson 7.

Interestingly, the word "patient" and the phrase "not a brawler" both have to do with *restraining one's emotions* and *controlling the tongue*. A leader who is "not a brawler" is *one who turns down opportunities to get caught up in a war of words*. Please refer back to Lesson 8 for more on these words.

Note: The words "not greedy of filthy lucre" do *not* appear in the original Greek text. However, the essence of what they communicate does appear at the end of the verse in the form of the phrase "not covetous." This is a translation of the word *aphilarguros*, which pictures *one who is free from the love of money; one who does not have a preoccupation with money or a fixation on material possessions*.

"One that ruleth well his own house, having his children in subjection with all gravity (For if a man know not how to rule his own house, how shall he take care of the church of God?)"

1 Timothy 3:4,5

In our last lesson, we learned that the word "ruleth" in verse 4 is the Greek word *proistimi*, and it describes *one who stands before others in order to lead, guide, direct, or manage a situation; one who is up front as a visible leader in the home to protect and to serve as a shield for others*.

The word "well" is the Greek word *kalos*, which means this person is *leading his home in a way that is viewed as good*. His actions are *well-perceived and appealing to others*. In fact, his leadership is so attractive that people are beginning to say, "Wow! I want a family and a home like that!"

This brings us to the word "house," which is the Greek word *oikos*. It describes not only *the family residents of the house*, but also *the physical house itself, including the management of the house, the bills, and everything that happens in a house as well as its physical state*. In other words, is the grass mowed? Are the dishes washed? Are the bills paid on time? Is the house in good condition or disrepair? And what is the state of the family members?

Paul added that a potential leader should have "…his children in subjection with all gravity." The word "children" is the Greek word *teknon*, which describes *children who are still under parental guidance at home*. The word "subjection" means *to set things in order; to be subject to a defined order*. It depicts *obedience to authority; one who is submitted to some type of authority and is expected to act according to that order of authority*. And the word "gravity" — the Greek word *semnotes* — pictures *one who carries himself with dignity and treats other people with courtesy and respect*.

Basically, Paul told Timothy, "Before you make a person a leader in the church, look at how they are leading in their own home. Are they out in front protecting and providing for their family? Are they taking care of the upkeep and repairs of their house? Are things orderly? Do they pay their bills on time? And are they teaching and instilling the importance of honor and respect for those in authority in their children?" If a potential leader is failing the test of leadership at home, how can he possibly do anything differently in the church? This is precisely what Paul wrote in First Timothy 3:5.

What Is the Meaning of the Word 'Novice'?

In First Timothy 3:6, Paul went on to say that a leader in the church should "Not [be] a novice, lest being lifted up with pride he fall into the condemnation of the devil." Now you may have heard that the word "novice" refers to a new believer, and in one respect that is true. The word "novice" is the Greek word *neophutos*, which means a *new plant*. This definition is likely from where the idea that a "novice" is a new convert or a new Christian originated.

However, there is a deeper meaning that must be taken into consideration. This *new plant* (novice) could also be a *transplant*. That is to say, while a plant may be new to a particular garden, it could also be a very old plant that has been removed from one place and transplanted into another. Thus, the word "novice" — the Greek word *neophutos* — could be translated as *a new arrival*. Basically, Paul told Timothy, "Be careful not to move too quickly and make a new arrival to your church a leader."

Imagine this: "Pastor John" is praying for God to send him more laborers to help with the harvest of souls (*see* Matthew 9:37,38). Suddenly someone special shows up in the church. "Larry," a veteran believer shows up, and he has worked with children, served as a deacon, and played multiple instruments on a worship team. He seems to be great with people and holds a high position in a growing corporation, which makes him a potentially large giver. On the surface, it seems as though Pastor John's prayers have been answered. Excited about the possibilities, he moves forward and places this new transplant into a visible position of leadership. Within a short time, Larry's mask comes off and an unsubmissive, controlling spirit comes out. What was thought to be a "dream come true" has quickly turned into a nightmare.

If only this pastor would have taken some time to pray and do some checking, he would have discovered that this "super Christian" was actually a dissatisfied, disgruntled individual who had been ping-ponging back and forth between churches for awhile. He had probably produced many of the same problems in the previous churches that were surfacing in the new one. This is exactly why Paul urged Timothy not to appoint a "novice" to a position of leadership.

In his book entitled *Promotion*, Rick offers some valuable insights he gained from dealing with novices[2]:

> When someone has a chronic pattern of moving from one church to another, you can be ninety-nine percent sure this person has some type of spiritual problem. If you talk to him, he will probably tell you why *none* of those churches was good enough. But all the churches in a city can't be wrong.

---

[2] Renner, Rick. Ten Guidelines To Help You Achieve Your Long-Awaited Promotion! Shippensburg, PA: Harrison House, 2000.

Be aware that a person who can't find a church good enough for him probably won't be pleased with your church either. Something is very wrong spiritually with this type of person.

I've discovered through the years that people who continually move from church to church are frequently judgmental, critical of leadership, and unwilling to submit to spiritual authority. That's why they never stay in one church very long....

...These floaters frequently tell the pastor, *'I love you. You are the best pastor in the city. I thank God for your ministry.'* They may even do fine in the church as long as the pastor doesn't talk about subjects such as *tithing, submission, authority, commitment*, or *money*. But as soon as the pastor touches on a subject that these people consider to be unspiritual or that rubs them the wrong way, they are out of the church and on their way to the next. One week earlier they loved the pastor, but now they're judging him as they walk out the door....

Unfortunately, the Body of Christ is filled with these kinds of people. Regardless of where you live, people who float from church to church will eventually find the path to your church as well — if they haven't already. You'll recognize them by their rebellion to authority, which is usually disguised under a mask of super-spirituality....

...This is the voice of experience speaking to you right now! Let me give you this recommendation: When a person comes to you from another church, don't use him at first. Even if you think his potential is great, first let him *prove* that he is really called to your church and submitted to your authority.

Tell him to sit under the Word for a while before he gets involved so he can know you and know your heart better. If he really is so *spiritual*, he should be able to recognize this as wise counsel.

Friend, if a believer has left another church and has come to your church, don't be too quick to lay hands on him and appoint him as a leader. Do some digging. Ask the person some probing questions, such as why he left his last church. If you're thinking about placing this individual in a key position, consider calling his previous pastor and asking him for input on the potential leader's character. This is not gossip. It is wisdom in action as you seek to protect your church.

Why Should a 'Novice' *Not* Be Made a Leader?

In the latter part of First Timothy 3:6, Paul gives us the reason we shouldn't make a "novice" a leader: "...lest being lifted up with pride he fall into the condemnation of the devil." The phrase "lifted up with pride" is a translation of the Greek word *tuphloo*, which means *blind*. What is interesting about this word is that it doesn't just depict a person who is unable to see, but *a person who has been intentionally blinded by someone else*. Specifically, it is one who has been blinded by his own conceit. He is so overly impressed with himself that he can no longer see himself for who he really is. This individual hasn't just lost his sight — he has no eyes to see.

The word *tuphloo* is also from where we derive the word "typhoon." The implication here is clear: If you quickly lay hands on a new believer or a newly transplanted person to your church and appoint him or her to be a leader, you will likely release a spiritual storm into your congregation. Most of these storms can be avoided by moving slower, asking probing questions, and proceeding with caution.

The Scripture goes on to say that the person who is blinded by their own conceit will "...fall into the condemnation of the devil" (1 Timothy 3:6). The words "fall into" is the Greek word *empipto*, which means *to fall into; to collapse into*. It pictures *a downward plummet into something* or *a fall into a terrible predicament*. It can also depict *someone who falls into some type of failure* or *a downfall from a presumed high and haughty position*.

This brings us to the word "condemnation," which is the Greek word *krima*, and it describes *a verdict; sentence; judgment;* or *condemnation*. In this particular verse, it describes what happened to the devil when he was kicked out of Heaven. The Bible says he became overly impressed with himself and began to desire the worship that rightfully belongs to God. In fact, he felt he was so magnificent that he deserved to be worshiped.

When a "novice" is promoted too quickly, the devil begins to work on their mind, and they fall into the same pattern of "condemnation," or judgment, of the devil. They begin to think things like, *Why should I be in submission to the pastor? Why should I submit to anyone? Am I not just as anointed as they are? Do I not hear from God as well as they do?* And just like Satan, their unchecked, unrepentant pride sets them up for a great downfall.

Potential Leaders Have a 'Good Report' — Even Among Unbelievers

The apostle Paul wraps up his list of qualifications for leaders in First Timothy 3:7, saying, "Moreover he [a leader] must have a good report of them which are without; lest he fall into reproach and the snare of the devil." The word "must" is the Greek word *dei* — the same word we saw in verse 2. It describes *an obligation or necessity; something that absolutely must be.*

Paul said a leader absolutely must "have" a good report. The word "have" in Greek is the word *echo*, which means *to hold; to have; to be in possession of.* The phrase "good report" in Greek is *marturian kalen*, and it means *a good testimony; a good witness; an appealing or attractive witness.* This attractive witness is "of them which are without." The word "of" is the Greek word *apo*, which means *coming from,* and the word "without" is the Greek word *exothen*, which describes *those on the outside; those outside of Christ.* This refers to *non-church members* or *non-Christians.*

So what are unbelievers saying about the person you are considering for leadership? If you yourself desire to be in leadership, what are unbelievers saying about *you?* We need to listen to what those outside of the church have to say about people's character. A good leader will even have a good reputation among unbelievers.

My friend, these are the qualifications for leadership. They are biblical, yet extremely practical. There is no mention of Bible school diplomas or seminary degrees — just everyday issues of good character and common sense. If you desire to be a visible leader in the house of God, you desire a good thing! And now you know the requirements to achieve your desire. May the Lord give you the grace you need to humbly serve and advance His Kingdom.

STUDY QUESTIONS

Study to shew thyself approved unto God, a workman that needeth not to be ashamed, rightly dividing the word of truth.
— 2 Timothy 2:15

1. Who can you think of in Scripture that had a "good reputation" among believers and non-believers alike? (Consider Proverbs 22:1; Romans 1:8; Acts 5:13,14.)

2. According to Psalm 92:12-15, what *blessings* can you expect from being *planted* in your local church? (Also consider Psalm 1:1-3; Jeremiah 17:7,8.)

3. The Bible talks about Satan's fall in Isaiah 14:12-17 and Ezekiel 28:13-19. Take time to reflect on these passages. What stands out most about Satan's character? Does anything in his reasoning or actions hit close to home? What can we learn *not* to do from watching his selfish ambition play out?

PRACTICAL APPLICATION

But be ye doers of the word, and not hearers only,
deceiving your own selves.
— James 1:22

1. Have you ever seen a novice be appointed to a position of leadership? If so, briefly describe what you observed. What were the "stormy" results you saw surrounding this individual?

2. Do you know of someone who tends to hop from church to church? What reasons has he given for not settling down and allowing God to plant him in one church body? Have *you* ever hopped from church to church? If so, take a moment to ask yourself why.

3. Imagine you're a leader at your church and you're interviewing a few people for potential leadership positions. What kind of questions could you ask to help reveal their true character, level of commitment, and ability to fit and to thrive on your team?